# A Marriage Sourcebook

# A Marriage Sourcebook

*Edited by*
J. Robert Baker
Joni Reiff Gibley
Kevin Charles Gibley

*Art by*
Meltem Aktaş

LITURGY
TRAINING
PUBLICATIONS

## Acknowledgments

We are grateful to the many publishers and authors who have given permission to include their work. Every effort has been made to determine the ownership of all texts and to make proper arrangements for their use. We will gladly correct in future editions any oversight or error that is brought to our attention.

Acknowledgments for sources not listed below will be found in the endnotes.

Scripture texts used in this text, except for the psalms, are taken from the New Revised Standard Version of the Bible, © 1989, Division of Christian Education of the National Coucil of the Churches of Christ in the United States of America. Published by Oxford University Press, Inc., 200 Madison Avenue, New York NY 10016. Used with permission. All rights reserved.

The English translation of the psalms from the *Liturgical Psalter,* © 1993, International Committee on English in the Liturgy, Inc. All rights reserved.

Excerpts from the English translation of the *The Roman Missal* © 1973, International Committee on English in the Liturgy (ICEL); excerpts from the English translation of *The Liturgy of the Hours,* © 1974, ICEL; excerpts from the English translation of *Rite of Marriage* © 1974, ICEL. All rights reserved.

Editor: Victoria M. Tufano
Permissions and copy editor: Jennifer McGeary
Editorial assistance: Lorraine Schmidt
Production: Judy Sweetwood
Typesetter: Kari Nicholls
Series designer: Michael Tapia

Copyright © 1994, Archdiocese of Chicago: Liturgy Training Publications, 1800 North Hermitage Avenue, Chicago IL 60622-1101; 1-800-933-1800, fax 1-800-933-7094; e-mail orders@ltp.org. All rights reserved.

Printed in the United States of America

05 04 03 02 01 00 99 98    7 6 5 4 3 2

MARRSB
ISBN 1-56854-039-6
Library of Congress Cataloging-in-Publication Data.
A marriage sourcebook / edited by J. Robert Baker, Joni Gibley, Kevin Charles Gibley ; art by Meltem Aktaş.

    p.   cm.
    ISBN 1-56854-039-6
    1. MARRIAGE — Religious aspects — Catholic Church.   2. Catholic Church — Liturgy.   3. Marriage service.   I. Baker, J. Robert, 1954-.   II. Gibley, Joni.   III. Gibley, Kevin Charles.
BX2250.M267   1994
264'.02085 — dc20

94-25324
CIP

# Contents

# Introduction

Marriage is unique among the sacraments in that each celebration may be fashioned, to a great extent, according to individual and cultural tastes. As ceremony, then, no two weddings are exactly the same; as lifelong sacrament, no two marriages are the same, either. The bride and groom participate in — no, co-celebrate — their sacrament, but it is a sacrament that, despite individual manners, signifies a universal union. The celebration of marriage, like all the sacraments, draws and holds the church together in the reaffirmation of our core beliefs. Marriage's celebration of the life of faith is a gift shared by all who witness it.

Three intersecting, complementary relationships lie at the heart of the sacrament of marriage: 1) the marital relationship, the joining of bride and groom; 2) the reliance on God shared by bride and groom; and 3) the bonds between the community gathered and the wedding couple. Fittingly, the circle is the symbol most often associated with the sacrament. Whether it is described by wedding rings, by crowns or by lassos, the circle operates as a symbol of constancy, a sign of the continuity and endurance promised on wedding days.

Because marriage, like all sacraments, enacts the words of liturgy, this book is organized around blessings and vows associated with various marriage rites, one of which begins each section of the book. This structure, though, is no more linear than the course of married life; the concerns of each invocation resound with the promises of the ones that precede it and the ones that succeed it. Similarly, marriage as it is lived is not a series of graduated steps where one vow, like some finite task, is mastered and then left behind. The rejoicing of the wedding must be woven into the fabric of the everyday, as each member both individually and jointly seeks to integrate — to knit — their wills together, and to the will of the Lord. The texts within and across each section bear the circle metaphor out, for the meditations gathered here continually return to and repeat common themes, like a wheel — or a ring — spun to catch the light of God's grace.

The circle that encompasses marriage as sacrament begins with the first meeting and initial steps of a committed love. Though it may not be good for the *adam* — the first human being — to be alone, the *adam* should not unite until the promise of fidelity for all the days to come can be vouchsafed. The Latin root of "fidelity," *fidelis,* boldly announces the compact of the marriage vows, a compact stitched together with threads of faith in one another and faith in God. The circle of marriage includes God, greeted with gratitude, who has bestowed love and union as gift.

Celebrating God's gift is a recurrent act. Just as we return again and again to the eucharist and the present reality of the Lord's sacrifice, so, too, do the bride and groom return to the presence of the Lord in their daily life. The spouse is a figure of God's presence, perpetual source of strength and comfort. In response, each spouse renews and reconsecrates the sacrament each morning, buoyed by constant growth in and with the other and God.

The marriage thus strengthened and renewed radiates out to extend the circle. Though the two are made one flesh, this union is but an indication of the larger marriage of God with humanity made manifest in community. As Christ is sign of sacrifice and faith in God's will, the wedded couple stands as sign of equally devoted love and of the promise of unity to come. The sign, though, is not static. The couple's love for one another grows and is reenacted with each new day; the love and unity they represent takes root in the fruits of the marriage — children, when God wills, and the circle of others reached out to from the grace and affection of the marriage union. The strength of the partnership, Rachel Reeder has written, "resides in the multiple relationships of the kingdom, for marriage is a sign of neighbor love as the eucharist is a sign of God's love."

The circle of marriage includes not only multiple neighbor relationships, but also a multileveled relationship between spouses — excluding no pain and no joy. The kingdom of heaven lies along the path of unity. While the path of marriage is often paved with joy, the journey is not always one of ease. Each marriage is fraught with the perils of detour and losing one's way; but the faults in the road are also shared, if not celebrated, as opportunities to repair and strengthen the bonds cemented by God's grace.

This book is offered in acknowledgment of both the joy and the struggle of marriage. Where love and honor are promised, the task can never be taken easily or lightly, but at its core, marriage is lifelong sacramental act which consecrates a covenant lived under the sign of, and as a sign of, God's grace and love.

Kevin and Joni Gibley

THE LORD God said, "It is not good that the man should be alone; I will make him a helper as his partner." So the LORD God caused a deep sleep to fall upon the man, and he slept; then he took one of his ribs and closed up its place with flesh. And the rib that the LORD God had taken from the man he made into a woman and brought her to the man. Then the man said,

"This at last is bone of my bones
  and flesh of my flesh;
this one shall be called Woman,
  for out of Man this one was taken."

Genesis 2:18, 21 – 23

BONE represents strength, flesh represents weakness. She will be part of him in both good times and bad. Humankind, the Hebrew saw, was fulfilled in the act of marriage. It was part of the blessedness of the world order.

Robert Crotty
and John Barry Ryan

THE masculine and feminine form the archetypal human monad: Adam-Eve. The Fall breaks up this oneness into a bad masculinity and a bad femininity: couples made of two polarized, objectified, and separate individuals, situated outside each other, placed nonetheless side by side. From this comes the distance itself between the two poles of human existence: either they are opposites marred by discord and a fruitless contention, or they are unlikes who accept one another, complementaries who love each other, the conjunction of opposites. The nuptial community arises as the prophetic figure of the Kingdom of God: the ultimate unity, the community of the Masculine and the Feminine in their totality in God.

Paul Evdokimov

SO when she speaks, the voice of Heaven I hear
So when we walk, nothing impure comes near;
Each field seems Eden, and each calm retreat;
Each village seems the haunt of holy feet.

*William Blake*
*Eighteenth century*

THE bee is mad without its honey
The cuckoo is mad without spring
And you being absent I am like them,
May God be my witness!

*Indian Dohā*

OUR mind's desire is to know, to understand;
but our heart's desire is intimacy, to be known,
to be understood.

*John S. Dunne*

EVERY deed and every relationship is surrounded by an
atmosphere of silence. Friendship needs no words — it is
solitude delivered from the anguish of loneliness.

*Dag Hammarskjöld*

LONELINESS clarifies. Here silence stands
Like heat. Here leaves unnoticed thicken,
Hidden weeds flower, neglected waters quicken,
Luminously-peopled air ascends;
And past the poppies bluish neutral distance
Ends the land suddenly beyond a beach
Of shapes and shingle. Here is unfenced existence:
Facing the sun, untalkative, out of reach.

*Philip Larkin*

God created co-being.

Cyril of Alexandria
Fifth century

Rabbi Hanilai said: A man who has no wife lives without joy, blessing and good. In the West they said, "Without Torah and without [moral] protection." Rabbi ben Ulla said, "And without peace."

Talmud

'Tis midnight, but small thoughts have I of sleep:
    Full seldom may my friend such vigils keep!
Visit her, gentle sleep! with wings of healing,
    And may this storm be but a mountain-birth,
May all the stars hang bright above her dwelling,
    Silent as though they watched the sleeping Earth!
        With light heart may she rise,
        Gay fancy, cheerful eyes,
    Joy lift her spirit, joy attune her voice;
To her may all things live from pole to pole,
Their life the eddying of her living soul!
    O simple spirit, guided from above,
Dear lady! friend devoutest of my choice
Thus mayest thou ever, evermore rejoice.

Samuel Taylor
Coleridge
Nineteenth century

When the black-lettered list to the gods was presented,
    (The list of what Fate for each mortal intends,)
At the long string of ills a kind goddess relented,
And slipped in three blessings—wife, children, and friends.

William Robert
Spencer

BLESS, O Lord, the wedlock of these persons through your mercy, as you blessed the wedlock of Abraham and Sarah, of Isaac and Rebekah, of Jacob and Rachel. And as you have said through the apostle: Honorable is wedlock and holy the bed. So keep holy the marriage bed of these persons and graciously bestow on them seed according to your will, that they may be blessed according to your word: Increase and multiply and replenish the earth. And increase them with the increment of holiness, to the end that their seed may become numerous upon the earth, and may become worthy of the adoption of your inheritance, glorying Father and Son and Holy Spirit, now and ever and Armenian liturgy    to eternity.

John Chrysostom
Fourth century    THE one who loves has another self.

LOVE and commitment, it appears, are desirable, but not easy. For, in addition to believing in love, we Americans Robert Bellah    believe in the self.

THE overtones are lost, and what is left are conversations which, in their poverty, cannot hide the lack of real contact. We glide past each other. Buy why? Why — ?

We reach out toward each other. In vain — because we Dag Hammarskjöld    have never dared to give ourselves.

STRANGE atoms we unto ourselves
    Soaring a strange demesne
    With life and death the darkened doors
Georgia Douglas
Johnson    And love the light between.

HE

B Y the clearing at the Eastern Gate
Where madder grows on the bank —
Strange that the house should be so near
Yet the person distant indeed!

SHE

By the chestnut-trees at the Eastern Gate
Where there is a row of houses.
It is not that I do not love you,
But that you are slow to court me.

Chou song
Seventh century BCE

T HERE are three possible parts to a date, of which at least
two must be offered, entertainment, food and affection.
It is customary to begin a series of dates with a great deal of
entertainment, a moderate amount of food and the merest
suggestion of affection. As the amount of affection increases,
the entertainment can be reduced proportionately. When
the affection *is* the entertainment, we no longer call it dat-
ing. Under no circumstances can the food be omitted.

Judith Martin

L OVE is principally made up of desire; and without desire
there would be but little tendency of the sexes for each
other's society. Thus nature was compelled to make love a
selfish pleasure, to the end of population.

Eugene Becklard
Nineteenth century

BETROTHAL was so important that, even though only the Coptic and Armenian rites have a full liturgy with lections, *each one* of the rites from the Armenian-Syrian family employs a special symbolism at betrothal, as if there were a need to make this rite significant in the lives of ordinary men and women. Thus, betrothed Armenian couples exchange crosses; the Syrian orthodox priest goes to the home of each partner to act as a sort of intermediary; the Maronites include an anointing of the couple (which they probably took from the Copts); and the East Syrians make a curious mixture of water, ash, and wine in a chalice (the *henana*) for the couple to drink, to symbolize the dying of the old relationship in order to come to life in the new.

Kenneth W. Stevenson

OVER the southern hill so deep
The male fox drags along,
But the way to Lu is easy and broad
For this Ch'i lady on her wedding-way.
Yet once she has made the journey,
Never again must her fancy roam.

When we plant hemp, how do we do it?
Across and along we put the rows.
When one takes a wife, how is it done?
The man must talk with her father and mother.
And once he has talked with them,
No one else must he court.

Chou song
Seventh century BCE

THE ancient Russian tradition viewed the time of engagement as a novitiate. After the marriage ceremony, a retreat in a monastery was prescribed for the newly married to prepare for entrance into their "nuptial priesthood."

Paul Evdokimov

LABAN and Bethuel answered, "The thing comes from the LORD; we cannot speak to you anything bad or good. Look, Rebekah is before you, take her and go, and let her be the wife of your master's son, as the LORD has spoken."

Genesis 24:50–51, 58–61

O God, who prospered the way of Abraham's steward when he went to take a wife for Isaac, his master's son, bless, O Lord, your worshipers' betrothal in the abundant grace of your mercies, and guard them by your cross from all harm.

Syrian Orthodox liturgy

CALL it neither love nor spring madness,
Nor chance encounter nor quest ended.
Observe it casually as pussy willows
Or pushcart pansies on a city street.
Let this seed growing in us
Granite-strong with persistent root
Be without name, or call it the first
Warm wind that caressed your cheek
And traded unshared kisses between us.
Call it the elemental earth
Bursting the clasp of too-long winter
And trembling for the plough-blade.

Let our blood chant it
And our flesh sing anthems to its arrival,
But our lips shall be silent, uncommitted.

Pauli Murray

TO marry, just as to become a monk, means to take an absolute risk.

Paul Evdokimov

THEIR eyes are big and blue with love; its lighting
    Makes even us look new: yes, today it all looks so easy.
  Will Ferdinand be as fond of a Miranda
Familiar as a stocking? Will a Miranda who is
    No longer a silly lovesick little goose,
When Ferdinand and his brave world are her profession,
    Go into raptures over existing at all?
Probably I over-estimate their difficulties;
    Just the same, I am very glad I shall never
Be twenty and have to go through that business again,
    The hours of fuss and fury, the conceit, the expense.

W. H. Auden

I really don't see anything romantic in proposing. It is very
romantic to be in love. But there is nothing romantic
about a definite proposal. Why, one may be accepted. One
usually is, I believe. Then the excitement is all over. The
very essence of romance is uncertainty.

Oscar Wilde
Nineteenth century

THERE are years that ask questions and years that answer.
    Janie had had no chance to know things, so she had to
ask. Did marriage end the cosmic loneliness of the
unmated? Did marriage compel love like the sun the day?

Zora Neale Hurston

ALTHOUGH I can at least confine
    Your vanity and mine
To stating timidly
A timid similarity,
We shall boast anyway:
Like love I say.

Like love we don't know where or why,
Like love we can't compel or fly,
Like love we often weep,
Like love we seldom keep.

W. H. Auden

THE problem with marriage is that it ends every night after making love, and it must be rebuilt every morning before breakfast.

Gabriel García
Márquez

LOVE, like martyrdom, cannot be imposed on someone. The promise of fidelity is borne on the deepest realities of human life and on transrational realities. It is not imposed from without but arises from within, from the heart's dimension, and is addressed to the freedom of the spirit like an invitation to a banquet and a call to suffering. The act of faith enters into it, and one's fidelity comes alive in accordance with the integrity of one's faith.

Paul Evdokimov

THUS piteously Love closed what he begat,
The union of this ever-diverse pair!
These two were rapid falcons in a snare,
Condemned to do the flitting of the bat.
Lovers beneath the singing sky of May,
They wandered once; clear as the dew on flowers.
But they fed not on the advancing hours:
Their hearts held cravings for the buried day.
Then each applied to each that fatal knife,
Deep questioning, which probes to endless dole.
Ah, what a dusty answer gets the soul
When hot for certainties in this our life!

In tragic hints here see what evermore
Moves dark as yonder midnight ocean's force,
Thundering like ramping hosts of warrior horse,
To throw that faint, thin line upon the shore!

George Meredith
Nineteenth century

How Love burns through the Putting in the Seed
On through the watching for that early birth
When, just as the soil tarnishes with weed,
The sturdy seedling with arched body comes
Shouldering its way and shedding the earth crumbs.

Robert Frost

'Tis a hazard both ways I confess, to live single or to marry, *Nam et uxorem ducere, et non ducere malum est,* it may be bad, it may be good, as it is a cross and calamity on the one side, so 'tis a sweet delight, an incomparable happiness, a blessed estate, a most unspeakable benefit, a sole content, on the other, 'tis all in the proof. Be not then so wayward, so covetous, so distrustful, so curious and nice, but let's all marry.

Robert Burton
Seventeenth century

Sometimes I feel thy cheek against my face
Close-pressing, soft as is the South's first breath
That all the subtle earth-things summoneth
To spring in woodland and in meadow space.

Yea sometimes in a bustling man-filled place
Meseemeth somewise thy hair wandereth
Across mine eyes, as mist that halloweth
The air awhile and giveth all things grace.

Or on still evenings when the rain falls close
There comes a tremor in the drops, and fast
My pulses run, knowing thy thought hath passed
That beareth thee as doth the wind a rose.

Ezra Pound

G ET up!
Get up out of the darkness!
Rouse yourself;
open the eye of your understanding
and look into the depth
within the deep well of divine charity.
For unless you see,
you cannot love.
The more you see,
the more you will love.
Once you love,
you will follow,
and you will clothe yourself in God's will.

Catherine of Siena
Fourteenth century

S O she got up, and they began to pray and implore that
they might be kept safe. Tobias began by saying,

"Blessed are you, O God of our ancestors,
    and blessed is your name in all generations forever.
Let the heavens and the whole creation
    bless you forever.
You made Adam, and for him you made his wife Eve
    as a helper and support.
    From the two of them the human race has sprung.
You said, 'It is not good that the man should be alone;
    let us make a helper for him like himself.'
I now am taking this kinswoman of mine,
    not because of lust,
    but with sincerity.
Grant that she and I may find mercy
    and that we may grow old together."

And they both said, "Amen, Amen."

Tobit 8:5 – 8

I take you to be my spouse. I promise to be true to you in good times and in bad, in sickness and in health. I will love you and honor you all the days of my life.

Roman liturgy

So God created humankind in his image,
in the image of God he created them;
male and female he created them.

Genesis 1:27

FROM the beginning of creation, "God made them male and female." "For this reason a man shall leave his father and mother and be joined to his wife, and the two shall become one flesh." So they are no longer two, but one flesh. Therefore what God has joined together, let no one separate.

Mark 10:6 – 9

ON that day, says the LORD, you will call me, "My husband," and no longer will you call me, "My Baal." For I will remove the names of the Baals from her mouth, and they shall be mentioned by name no more. I will make for you a covenant on that day with the wild animals, the birds of the air, and the creeping things of the ground; and I will abolish the bow, the sword, and war from the land; and I will make you lie down in safety. And I will take you for my wife forever; I will take you for my wife in righteousness and in justice, in steadfast love, and in mercy. I will take you for my wife in faithfulness; and you shall know the LORD.

Hosea 2:16 – 20

THE basic pillars of the marriage, as reflected in the classic verse of betrothal uniting God with the community of Israel, are that it be forever, that it combine righteousness and proper behavior together with kindness and mercifulness, and that it be a union fused in faith.

*Forever* speaks of the unconditionality of commitment to the marriage. *Righteousness and proper behavior* refers to the legal framework of the marriage, *kindness and mercifulness* to the sensitive manner with which the legal framework is permeated. *A union fused in faith* relates to a match in which the couple have faith that each is for the other, in the ultimate shared-destiny sense.

Reuven P. Bulka

BE it known to all here present that N., son of N., of the parish of N., and N., daughter of N., of the parish of N., intend to be united in holy matrimony. Wherefore, we hereby admonish each and all that, if anyone of you has knowledge of an impediment of blood relationship, relationship through marriage, spiritual relationship, or of any other kind, you are bound to make it known to the pastor or the bishop as soon as possible. This is the first publication of the banns.

*Roman Ritual*

LET me not to the marriage of true minds
Admit impediments. Love is not love
Which alters when it alteration finds,
Or bends with the remover to remove:
Oh, no! it is an ever-fixéd mark,
That looks on tempests and is never shaken;
It is the star to every wandering bark,
Whose worth's unknown, although his height be taken.
Love's not Time's fool, though rosy lips and cheeks
Within his bending sickle's compass come;
Love alters not with his brief hours and weeks,
But bears it out even to the edge of doom.
If this be error and upon me proved,
I never writ, nor no man ever loved.

William Shakespeare
Sixteenth century

COULD I have this dance for the rest of my life?
Would you be my partner ev'ry night?
When we're together, it feels so right.
Could I have this dance for the rest of my life?

*Wayland Holyfield
and Bob House*

I take the
to haue and to holde
(from this day forward),
for better for wurs,
for rycher for porer,
in syckenes and in helthe,
to be bonoure and buxum,
in bed and at borde,
tyll deth us depart
(yf holy Chyrche will it ordeyn)
and thereto I plyght the my trouth.

*The Sarum Manual*

BEYOND obedience, its attention fixed on the goal — freedom from fear.

Beyond fear — openness to life.
And beyond that — love.

*Dag Hammarskjöld*

INSTEAD of consent being expressed explicitly or implicitly by an informal rite of betrothal, or even by the giving of a ring, from the twelfth century it becomes standard practice for all those seeking the blessing of the church on their union to have to stand at the church door and say, in the mother-tongue, that they want each other.

*Mark Searle*

MARRIAGES should not be contracted secretly, nor after dinner. But the bride and groom should fast and be blessed by a priest, also fasting, in a monastery. And before they are joined in wedlock, diligent inquiry is to be made concerning their family.

*Provincial Synod
of Rouen*

*Eleventh century*

MISS Manners has no objection to bridal couples' doing some discreet editing of the standard ceremony, omitting details they find offensive, such as obeying and giving away. Certainly the innovation of including children from previous unions who will be underfoot in the new one is important. But they should bear in mind that symbols are intended to apply generally to the social function of the occasion, and are not clues to private behavior. The bride and bridegroom should not use the occasion to announce that they have considered themselves married already, belittling the social and legal sanction they are now receiving. It is rude to brag about your sex life at a public function.

Traditional ceremonies, whether civil or religious, express hopes and ideals; they do not make realistic predictions. Statistically, it may be true that it is likely to be the bride and bridegroom's subsequent feelings, not death, which do them part. But that is no excuse for making lukewarm vows to stay together "as long as we both shall wish."

Judith Martin

MAKE of our hands one hand,
Make of our hearts one heart.
Make of our vows one last vow:
Only death will part us now.

Steven Sondheim

MAY almighty God,
who created our first parents, Adam and Eve,
sanctified them with a divine blessing
and joined them in a holy union,
sanctify and bless your hearts and bodies
and conjoin you in a union of true love.

Benedictional of
Robert of Jumieges

DO all to the honor and the glory of God.
Keep an eye ever single and free,
Thus ye shall see the truth of my word,
Christ's kingdom shall come unto thee.

*Shaker hymn*

CHRISTIAN love is, in the view of its practitioners, built of solider stuff than personal happiness or enjoyment. It is, first, a commitment, a form of obedience to God's word. In addition, love rests less on feeling than on decision and action. Real love may even, at times, require emotional self-denial, pushing feelings to the back in order to live up to one's commitments. Most critical in love are a firm decision about where one's obligations lie and a willingness to fulfill those obligations in action, independent of the ups and downs of one's feelings.

*Robert Bellah*

THINE..." A sacrifice — and a liberation — to obey a will for which "I" is in no respect a goal!

*Dag Hammarskjöld*

GRANT us, we beseech thee, O Lord, grace to follow thee whithersoever thou goest. In little daily duties to which thou callest us, bow down our wills to simple obedience, patience under pain or provocation, strict truthfulness of word or manner, humility and kindness. In great acts of duty or perfection, if thou shouldst call us to them, uplift us to sacrifice and heroic courage; that in all things, both small and great, we may be imitators of thy dear Son, even Jesus Christ our Lord.

*Christina Rossetti*
*Nineteenth century*

Most gracious God, we give you thanks for your tender love in sending Jesus Christ to come among us, to be born of a human mother, and to make the way of the cross to be the way of life. We thank you, also, for consecrating the union of man and woman in his name. By the power of your Holy Spirit, pour out the abundance of your blessing upon this man and this woman. Defend them from every enemy. Lead them into all peace. Let their love for each other be a seal upon their hearts, a mantle about their shoulders, and a crown upon their foreheads. Bless them in their work and in their companionship; in their sleeping and in their waking; in their joys and in their sorrows; in their life and in their death. Finally, in your mercy, bring them to that table where your saints feast for ever in your heavenly home; through Jesus Christ our Lord, who with you and the Holy Spirit lives and reigns, one God, for ever and ever.

*Book of Common Prayer*

Marriage is that relation between man and woman in which the independence is equal, the dependence mutual, and the obligation reciprocal.

*Louis Kaufman Anspacher*

That the mere glimpse of a plain cap
Could harry me with such longing,
Cause pain so dire!

That the mere glimpse of a plain coat
Could stab my heart with grief!
Enough! Take me with you to your home.

That a mere glimpse of plain leggings
Could tie my heart in tangles!
Enough! Let us two be one.

*Chou song*
*Seventh century BCE*

L OVE, according to the song, is loneliness, and loneliness is love, a longing for communion with another. There is a depth of loneliness that remains untouched, though, even when one is communing with another human being. That loneliness can become love too, can become a longing for communion with God.

John S. Dunne

# A s a Possible Lover

Practices
silence, the way of wind
bursting
its early lull. Cold morning
to night, we go so
slowly, without
thought
to ourselves. (Enough
to have thought
tonight, nothing
finishes it. What
you are, will have
no certainty, or
end. That you will
stay, where you are,
a human gentle wisp
of life. Ah . . .)
    practices
loneliness,
as a virtue. A single
specious need
to keep
what you have
never really
had.

Amiri Baraka
(LeRoi Jones)

LOVE may be like water.... And what person has never cupped water in the hand and looked into it, trying to know water? The water always has been dipped from a greater body. But humans are driven creatures, driven to know the world around and within them, and we feel the water's wetness, we gaze down into its clearness and taste the sweetness of it on our tongues. And resources exhausted, we must nod and look at the captive water in the cup of our hand and must say: "Yes, now I know water."

But who has held water in the hand forever? The water drops or is flung away and returns always and forever to the greater body. Captive water is subtly changed. To know water requires that all water be known — water in dew and water in oceans; water in high and lonely lakes and swift water, changing; water in branch and brook, scummed pond and foaming race; all water in water form and then to sense the water that is ice, tears, blood. And having come to know so much of water to know that there is still to be known the vast, dark rushing deep within the earth where the rivers run unseen.

I think love is like water... because it can't be held, and I think most of us seal and stop ourselves, making ourselves to be vessels instead of fountains.

Water or love held within a vessel always is longing to return to the greater body, and this inner longing in the human vessel is a suffering. There can be no human being so stoical who will not cry out sometime over such suffering, and try to explain this peculiar agony. We must see our relationship to our suffering and our yearning, and all our yearnings to express what we are to a woman, a man, a nation, a child, a gun, a dog, a piece of land or a house. All must be reduced to a single sound — love.

I'd like all children to know that a person is not a vessel, all closed, but a fountain and that love flows like water, flows through the fountain, returning always to the greater body and again to the fountain. What I want all children to know, I guess, is that we can not ever love one person deeply — spouse, child or friend — until we love everyone a little.       Prentiss Combs

WE press body against body — bringing to nought that human beauty which is only physical in that the surfaces of the body are animated by a spirit inaccessible to physical touch.

*Dag Hammarskjöld*

THOUGHT cleaves the interstellar gloom
And sits in Sirius' disc all night,
Till day makes him retrace his flight,
With smell of burning on every plume,
Back past the sun to an earthly room.

His gains in heaven are what they are.
Yet some say Love by being thrall
And simply staying possesses all
In several beauty that Thought fares far
To find fused in another star.

*Robert Frost*

BEHOLD, thou art consecrated unto me by this ring, according to the law of Moses and of Israel.

*Jewish liturgy*

WHY does almost everyone choose the third finger, left hand for the wedding ring? Ages ago it was believed that a certain vein ran directly from this finger to the heart, thus the third finger was closest to the seat of love.

*Howard Kirschenbaum and Rockwell Stensrud*

B<small>Y</small> a ring power was given to Joseph in Egypt;
by a ring Daniel was glorified in the land of Babylon;
by a ring the uprightness of Tamar was revealed;
by a ring our heavenly Father showed his bounty upon
      his Son,
for he said:
Bring the fatted calf and kill it,
and let us eat and make merry.
By your own right hand, O Lord,
you armed Moses in the Red Sea;
by your true word the heavens were established,
and the foundations of the earth were made firm;
and the right hands of your servants
also shall be blessed by your mighty word
and by your upraised arm.
Therefore, O Master,
bless now this putting-on of rings
with your heavenly blessing,
and let your angel go before them
all the days of their life.

Byzantine liturgy

T<small>HE</small> two rings are placed in the heart of the sanctuary, on
the altar table; thus they are touching the mystery of the
Kingdom and, as symbols of a new destiny, they indicate the
dimension into which the sacrament will lead the couple.     Paul Evdokimov

OLord, Jesus Christ, Bridegroom of truth and justice, you betrothed to yourself the church of the Gentiles and by your blood you wrote the deed of dowry, and by your nails you gave her a ring. As the ring of the holy church was blessed, bless now, O Lord, these rings that we give to your servant and your maid. This is the ring by which Sarah was betrothed to Abraham, Rebecca to Isaac, and Rachel to Jacob. By this ring all the power and authority over Egypt was placed in the hands of Joseph. By its surety Daniel was delivered and became great in the king's presence. By this ring the prodigal son was accepted. By the truth of this ring the just gained victory, and by its fame the merchants became rich. Great, therefore, is the pledge of this ring. This is the ring which invites the races and generations to the betrothals and wedding feasts and gathers them that are far, and mutual relations are accomplished between them. By this ring women are betrothed to men. By this ring the bridegrooms and the brides are joined in marriage. Bless, my Lord, these rings that they may become the sign and seal of the true betrothal of our daughter to our son. May they receive heavenly blessings and bring forth righteous sons and daughters. By your grace, O Lord, let their promise come to happy fulfillment. Rejoicing and exulting, let them offer praise and glory to you now and evermore. Amen.

Syrian Orthodox liturgy

LET me explain to you the true situation more fully, my child. I have given her to seven men of our kinsmen, and all died on the night when they went in to her. But now, my child, eat and drink, and the Lord will act on behalf of you both." But Tobias said, "I will neither eat nor drink anything until you settle the things that pertain to me." So Raguel said, "I will do so. She is given to you in accordance with the decree in the book of Moses, and it has been decreed

from heaven that she be given to you. Take your kinswoman; from now on you are her brother and she is your
sister. She is given to you from today and forever. May the
Lord of heaven, my child, guide and prosper you both this
night and grant you mercy and peace." Then Raguel summoned his daughter Sarah. When she came to him he took
her by the hand and gave her to Tobias, saying, "Take her to
be your wife in accordance with the law and decree written
in the book of Moses. Take her and bring her safely to your
father. And may the God of heaven prosper your journey
with his peace." Then he called her mother and told her to
bring writing material; and he wrote out a copy of a marriage contract, to the effect that he gave her to him as wife
according to the decree of the law of Moses. Then they
began to eat and drink.                                    Tobit 7:10d – 14

N OT with my hands
But with my heart I bless you:
May peace forever dwell
Within your breast!

May Truth's white light
Move with you and possess you —
And may your thoughts and words
Wear her bright crest!

May Time move down
Its endless path of beauty
Conscious of you
And better for your being!

Spring after Spring
Array itself in splendor
Seeking the favor
Of your sentient seeing!                          Donald Jeffrey Hayes

THE most ancient and universal symbol of the marriage union was holding hands. In many cultures a couple could not hold hands until they were officially wed. Even if a wedding contained no verbal vows, the simple act of hand holding was often enough to make the marriage valid. And since antiquity, holding hands, if only to exchange rings, has been part of almost every marriage service on earth. Today we have rings, legal certificates, and vows to show the world a couple is married, but the natural, affectionate hand holding by a couple in love still says much more.

Howard Kirschenbaum
and Rockwell Stensrud

IT seems as though the garden which you love
Were like a swinging censer, its incense
Floating before us as a reverent act
To sanctify and bless our night of love.
Tell me once more you love me, that 'tis you
Yes, really you, I touch, so, with my hand;
And tell me it is by your own free will
That you are here, and that you like to be
Just here, with me, under this sailing pine.
I need to hear it often for my heart
Doubts naturally, and finds it hard to trust.
Ah, Dearest, you are good to love me so,
And yet I would not have it goodness, rather
Excess of selfishness in you to need
Me through and through, as flowers need the sun.
I wonder can it really be that you
And I are here alone, and that the night
Is full of hours, and all the world asleep,
And none can call to you to come away;
For you have given all yourself to me
Making me gentle by your willingness.

Amy Lowell

THE wedding of the first couple was celebrated with pomp never repeated in the whole course of history since. God, before presenting Eve to Adam, attired and adorned her as a bride and appealed to the angels, saying: "Come, let us perform services of friendship for Adam and his helpmate, for the world rests upon friendly services, and they are more pleasing in my sight than the sacrifices Israel will offer upon the altar." The angels accordingly surrounded the marriage canopy, and God pronounced the blessings upon the bridal couple, as the *hazzan* does under the *huppah*. The angels then danced and played upon musical instruments before Adam and Eve in their ten chambers of gold, pearls, and precious stones, which God had prepared for them.

Pirke de Rabbi Eliezer
Rabbinic literature

ADORNED and crowned, I'd have her come,
   With all her queenly grace,
And mid my lords and mighty men
   Unveil her lovely face.

Each gem that sparkles in my crown,
   Or glitters on my throne,
Grows poor and pale when she appears,
   My beautiful, my own!

Frances E. W. Harper
Nineteenth century

THERE was a woman in Sidon, who lived ten years with her husband, and had borne no child. They went to Rabbi Simeon ben Yohai, and asked to be divorced. He said to them, "As your coming together was with a banquet, so let your separation be with a banquet." They agreed, and made for themselves a holiday and a banquet, and she made her husband drink more than enough. When his mind returned to him, he said to her, "My daughter, look out what is most precious to you in my house, and take it, and go to your father's house." What did she do? When he had gone to sleep, she beckoned to her servants and handmaids, and said to them, "Carry him on the mattress to my father's house." In the middle of the night he woke up, and he said to her, "Whither have I been brought?" She said, "To the house of my father." He said to her, "What have I to do there?" She said, "Did you not tell me last night to take what was most precious to me from your house, and to go with it to the house of my father? There is nothing in the world more precious than you."

*Talmud*

HE drifted off into sleep and Janie looked down on him and felt a self-crushing love. So her soul crawled out from its hiding place.

*Zora Neale Hurston*

YOU begin your married life by the voluntary and complete surrender of your individual lives in the interest of that deeper and wider life which you are to have in common. Henceforth you belong entirely to each other; you will be one in mind, one in heart, and one in affections. And whatever sacrifices you may hereafter be required to make to preserve this common life, always make them generously. Sacrifice is usually difficult and irksome. Only love can make it easy; and perfect love can make it a joy.

*Roman liturgy*

L ET me finish what I have been permitted to begin.
Let me give all without any assurance of increase.    Dag Hammarskjöld

T HE glory that you have given me I have given them, so
that they may be one, as we are one, I in them and you
in me, that they may become completely one, so that the
world may know that you have sent me and have loved
them even as you have loved me. Father, I desire that those
also, whom you have given me, may be with me where I
am, to see my glory, which you have given me because you
loved me before the foundation of the world.

Righteous Father, the world does not know you, but I know
you; and these know that you have sent me. I made your
name known to them, so that the love with which you have
loved me may be in them, and I in them.    John 17:22–26

LOOK with favor upon the world you have made, and for which your Son gave his life, and especially upon this man and this woman whom you make one flesh in holy matrimony.

*Book of Common Prayer*

LO, brethren, we are comen here
before God and his angels and all his halowes,
in the face and presence of our moder holy Chyrche,
for to couple and to knyt these two bodyes togyder,
that is to saye, of this man and of this woman,
that they be from this tyme forth
but one body and two soules
in the faythe and lawe of God and holy Chyrche,
for to deserve everylastynge lyfe,
what soever that they have done here before.

*The Sarum Manual*

SOME Pharisees came to Jesus, and to test him they asked, "Is it lawful for a man to divorce his wife for any cause?" He answered, "Have you not read that 'the one who made them at the beginning made them male and female' and said, 'For this reason a man shall leave his father and mother and be joined to his wife, and the two shall become one flesh'? So they are no longer two, but one flesh. Therefore what God has joined together, let no one separate.

Matthew 19:3 – 6

AT the beginning of the Ethiopic rite, the priest cuts a piece of hair from the bridegroom's head and places it on the bride's, and then cuts some of the bride's hair and places it on the groom's head. This is yet one more curious custom, symbolizing in one more way the union of the couple.

Kenneth W. Stevenson

HUSBAND and wife are like two wheels in the cart of life; and vainly will one try to draw it without the help of the other.

Lakshmi Bai Tilak

THE wedding ring symbolizes a "binding union" in marriage — but in earlier centuries, the binding was literal. In many cultures, a central part of the wedding ceremony consisted of tying some object on the bride and groom. Some tribes used grass, weeds, animal skins, hair, or other natural materials. In one tribe, rings of grass were tied on each partner, and later in the ceremony the rings were joined, binding the two together until the wedding was over. Along with hand holding, tying some object to both bride and groom appears to have been a universal practice. Even into the nineteenth century in several European countries a couple's hands were bound together all through their wedding. What better way can one think of for advertising a marriage than having two people roped together?

Howard Kirschenbaum
and Rockwell Stensrud

MOREOVER, those who are married are joined, after the blessing of the levite, by a single cord, and they should in no way disrupt the compact of marital unity. The cord they wear is woven of white and purple colors: the white standing for purity of life, the purple for the blood of [bearing] children. Thus this sign gives a warning that the rule of continence is to be kept by both partners for a while and that the marital debt is not hereafter to be withheld. This is what the Apostle enjoined on married people: "Keep continent for a while, that you may give yourselves to prayer" (1 Corinthians 7:5) — this is signified by the white in the cord — and then he adds "and then return to one another," which is signified by the purple color.

Isidore of Seville
Seventh century

Y ARD sale—Recently married couple is combining households. All duplicates will be sold, except children.

O perfect Love, all human thought transcending,
    Lowly we kneel in prayer before thy throne,
That theirs may be the love that knows no ending,
    Whom thou for evermore dost join in one.

O perfect Life, be thou their full assurance.
    Of tender charity and steadfast faith,
Of patient hope, and quiet, brave endurance,
    With childlike trust that fears nor pain nor death.

Grant them the joy which brightens earthly sorrow;
    Grant them the peace which calms all earthly strife,
And to life's day the glorious unknown morrow
    That dawns upon eternal love and life.

Dorothy F. Gurney
Nineteenth century

B LESS them, O Lord our God,
    as thou didst bless Abraham and Sarah.
Bless them, O Lord our God,
    as thou didst bless Isaac and Rebecca.
Bless them, O Lord our God,
    as thou didst bless Jacob and all the patriarchs.
Bless them, O Lord our God,
    as thou didst bless Joseph and Aseneth.
Bless them, O Lord our God,
    as thou didst bless Moses and Zipporah.
Bless them, O Lord our God,
    as thou didst bless Joachim and Anna
Bless them, O Lord our God,
    as thou didst bless Zechariah and Elizabeth.

Byzantine liturgy

THUS each new couple takes its place in the succession of generations, hopeful of doing its duty by God's grace, and of being blessed with children and an old age in which they see the succession continued in their children's children, before they pass to their reward. Even more than that, the whole succession of generations is somehow summed up in this bridal pair: in a certain sense, they *become* Adam and Eve, Abraham and Sarah, and the rest. They become more than themselves, assuming a role which transcends their individual lives and loves and faith: they become Everyman and Everywoman, the archetypal Man and Woman, king and queen, icons of the holy nation wedded to God.

Mark Searle

MARRIAGE belongs to the order of creation and to the order of redemption.

Walter Kasper

O may Thy holy spirit rest
upon this chosen few;
and give us fervency of heart,
thy perfect will to do.
We ask the gift of wisdom,
the precious boon of love,
the chain of spirit union
that links with worlds above.

Shaker hymn

LOOK down from heaven with favor, Lord, upon this union, and bestow thy blessing. And as thou didst send thy Angel Raphael as a harbinger of peace to Tobias and Sarah, the daughter of Raguel, so too graciously bless, O Lord, this husband and wife, that they may abide in thy blessing, persist in thy will, and live in thy love. Through Christ our Lord. Amen.

Roman liturgy

A group of people who have been to a wedding are on their way home. One says, "It was a beautiful wedding. I liked the food." Another says, "It was a great wedding. The music was marvelous." Still another one says, "It was the best wedding I ever went to. I saw all my good friends there and we had a terrific time." Reb Nachman, who has overheard them, says, "Those people weren't really at a wedding."

Then another wedding guest joins this group and says, *"Baruch HaShem!* Blessed be the Name! Thank God those two got together!" At that Reb Nachman says, "Now, *that* person was at a wedding!"

*Reb Nachman of Bratslav
Seventeenth century*

ALLELUIA and glory to you, Lord, Christ, Spouse who was invited to the wedding in Cana of Galilee, who blessed the bridegroom and bride and made their good abound; in your mercy may your right hand, filled with all spiritual goodness, be placed also on the bridegroom and bride, and bless them at the same time, so that they may sing your glory, and that of your blessed Father and Holy and life-giving Spirit, Alleluia, Alleluia!

*Maronite liturgy*

PRAISED are you, Lord our God, who has given us a vision of the paradise we dream of creating with our lives, and called it redemption. We praise you, O Lord, who created the commitment of marriage as a foretaste of redemption.

*Jewish liturgy*

O God,
through you a woman is joined to her husband
and society is chiefly ordered by that blessing
which was neither lost by original sin
nor washed away in the flood.

*Gregorian Sacramentary*

YOU are members of Christ through baptism. And now in Christ's name you are administering the sacrament of matrimony to each other, that by your sacred bond a new cell may be formed within his body, the church, to the advantage both of human society and the kingdom of God.    Roman liturgy

I bow my knees before the Father, from whom every family in heaven and on earth takes its name. I pray that, according to the riches of his glory, he may grant that you may be strengthened in your inner being with power through his Spirit, and that Christ may dwell in your hearts through faith, as you are being rooted and grounded in love.    Ephesians 3:14 – 17

WITH the love of the one who knows all,
With the patience of the one whose now is eternal,
With the righteousness of the one who has never failed,
With the humility of the one who has suffered all the
    possibilities of betrayal.    Dag Hammarskjöld

WHATEVER regard Christian people have for marriage in this age and whatever it proves to be in actual experience among the married, holy matrimony in its very essence is part and parcel of the "new creation" resulting from the espousal of God's eternal Son with his human creatures. For the members of Christ it is above all else a sacrament, and somewhat like the consecratory sacraments which imprint a character, matrimony constitutes a Christian couple in a new relationship to Christ and to his bride, the church.    Philip T. Weller

OUR mothers Rebekkah and Rachel
were betrothed and began new lives
at the gently flowing water of the well.
Our mother Yochevet
gave life to her child Moses in the
ever-flowing waters of the Nile.
Our sister Miriam
danced for the saving of lives
beside the
overflowing water
of the Sea of Reeds.

As Moses and Aaron
and the priests of Israel
washed with cleansing waters
before attending to God's service
at the altar,
So I now cleanse myself
before your altar of sanctification.

I am now prepared to shed
the impurities of my earlier life;
to become one with another life,
to become a creator of new life,
to become a partner in sharing the joys of life,
to teach and to learn
the lessons of married life.

Barbara Rosman
Penzner and Amy
Zwiback-Levenson

MAY each have for the other an undivided love
on which their union will stand and be strong.
Build them up on the foundation of your holy church,
that they may walk together in peace and harmony,
sealed by the word they have pledged to each other.
For you yourself are this bond of love
and the law which will guide their union.
May they be one in the union of their two persons,
according to your word.

Coptic liturgy

THE foundation for one's marriage actually begins at birth
and continues throughout life as one passes through
its different stages. Jesus, the carpenter's son, warns that
there are firm foundations and shifting ones. One builds
firmly when one acts upon Jesus' words. Every marriage of
Christians, therefore, will take into account the gospel and
its demands, not as something added to married life, but as
something that transforms married life from its destructive
possibilities into the dwelling place of generous love.

Robert Crotty and
John Barry Ryan

ON those who at thine altar kneel,
    O Lord, thy blessing pour,
That each may wake the other's zeal
    To love thee more and more:
O grant them here in peace to live,
    In purity and love,
And, this world leaving, to receive
    A crown of life above.

Adelaide Thrupp and
Godfrey Thring
Nineteenth century

O Lord, who did adorn the sky with luminaries: the sun, the moon, and the stars; O God, who did crown the earth with fruits, flowers and blossoms of all kinds; O Jesus Christ, who did crown kings, priests and prophets; O Compassionate One, who did bestow his triumph upon his worshipers in return for their heroic combat to keep the faith; Lord, who crowned king David with the crown of victory; O God, who encircled the ocean like a crown around all the earth; O Good One, who blessed the year by your grace, put your right hand, full of mercy and compassion, upon the heads upon which these crowns are placed. Grant them that they also may crown their children with righteousness, justice and mirth. May your peace and concord abide with them throughout their lives forever.

Syrian Orthodox liturgy

THE Lord is my shepherd, all that I need,
giving me rest in green and pleasant fields,
reviving my life by finding fresh water,
guiding my ways with a shepherd's care.

Though I should walk in death's dark valley,
I fear no evil with you by my side,
your shepherd's staff comforts me.

You spread my table in sight of my foes,
anoint my head, my cup runs over;
you tend me with love always loyal.

Psalm 23    I dwell with you, Lord, as long as I live.

MAY the blessing
which God poured out on Jacob through Isaac
descend upon you in all its fullness.
May the blessing
which Jacob invoked upon his beloved children
be increased when God gives it to you.
May the blessing
which Moses pronounced over the children of Israel
attend, by the favor of Christ,
upon your hearts;
and just as the redeemer of all,
our Lord Jesus Christ,
gave the fullness of his blessing
to the disciples,
so may he also cause that same blessing
to abound in your minds and bodies.                    Sacramentary of Vich

MAY we stay well in this country; we did not know that
we would arrive here. May we stay with peace and
dream honey; the God of old, the sun, when it rises in the
east, may it bring us honey, and when it goes to set in the     Prayer of the Nyole
west may it take the badness with it.                    Kenya

MAY all evil spirits be turned back from this place and
may the angels take up their awaited station here.        *Liber Ordinum*

GOD shields you,
a protector by your side.
The sun shall not harm you by day
nor the moon at night.

God shelters you from evil,
securing your life.
God watches over you near and far,
now and always.

Psalm 121:5 – 8

THE bridegroom is like the sun, the bride is like the moon, and all the wedding symbolizes the dawn which gladdens the earth.

Syrian Orthodox liturgy

SHE was stretched on her back beneath the pear tree soaking in the alto chant of the visiting bees, the gold of the sun and the panting breath of the breeze when the inaudible voice of it all came to her. She saw a dust-bearing bee sink into the sanctum of a bloom; the thousand sister-calyxes arch to meet the love embrace and the ecstatic shiver of the tree from root to tiniest branch creaming in every blossom and frothing with delight. So this was a marriage! She had been summoned to behold a revelation.

Zora Neale Hurston

NORMAL sex life, as a shared experience with apparently similar aims, further strengthens the feeling of unity and identity. This state is described as one of complete harmony, and is extolled as a great happiness ("one heart and one soul") — not without good reason, since the return to that original condition of unconscious oneness is like a return to childhood. Hence the childish gestures of all lovers. Even more is it a return to the mother's womb, into the teeming depths of an as yet unconscious creativity. It is, in truth, a genuine and incontestable experience of the Divine, whose transcendent force obliterates and consumes everything individual; a real communion with life and the impersonal power of fate.

Carl Jung

THE body of someone we love is not altogether naked,
but clothed and framed in our feelings.
                                        Anatole Broyard

THE fire of the body
burns away its dross and, rising in a flame of
self-surrender, consumes its closed microcosm.
                                        Dag Hammarskjöld

LOVE is not love until love's vulnerable.
She slowed to sigh, in that long interval.
A small bird flew in circles where we stood;
The deer came down, out of the dappled wood.
All who remember, doubt. Who calls that strange?
I tossed a stone, and listened to its plunge.
She knew the grammar of least motion, she
Lent me one virtue, and I live thereby.
                                        Theodore Roethke

PEOPLE should love their spouses as much as they love
themselves, not merely because they share the same
nature; no, the obligation is far greater, because there are no
longer two bodies, but one.
                                        John Chrysostom
                                        Fourth century

WE become the image of our own love, even in external appearance.
                                        Emanuel Swedenborg
                                        Eighteenth century

YOU are a part of me. I do not know
    By what slow chemistry you first became
A vital fiber of my being. Go
Beyond the rim of time or space, the same
Inflections of your voice will sing their way
Into the depths of my mind still. Your hair
Will gleam as bright, the artless play
Of word and glance, gesture and the fair
Young fingers waving, have too deeply etched
The pattern of your soul on mine. Forget
Me quickly as a laughing picture sketched
On water, I shall never know regret
Knowing no magic ever can set free
That part of you that is a part of me.

Frank Yerby

LOVE creates a dilemma for Americans. In some ways, love is the quintessential expression of individuality and freedom. At the same time, it offers intimacy, mutuality and sharing. In the ideal love relationship, these two aspects of love are perfectly joined — love is both absolutely free and completely shared. Such moments of perfect harmony among free individuals are rare, however. The sharing and commitment in a love relationship can seem, for some, to swallow up the individual, making her (more often than him) lose sight of her own interests, opinions and desires. Paradoxically, since love is supposed to be a spontaneous choice by free individuals, someone who has "lost" herself cannot really love, or cannot contribute to a real love relationship.

Robert M. Bellah

THEY were like those double stars which revolve round and round each other, and from a distance appear to be one. The absolute solitude in which they lived intensified their reciprocal thoughts; yet some might have said that it had the disadvantage of consuming their mutual affections at a fearfully prodigal rate. Yeobright did not fear for his own part; but recollection of Eustacia's old speech about the evanescence of love, now apparently forgotten by her, sometimes caused him to ask himself a question; and he recoiled at the thought that the quality of finiteness was not foreign to Eden.

Thomas Hardy
Nineteenth century

THEY come to be made into one body. See the mystery of love! If the two do not become one, they cannot increase; they can increase only by decreasing! How great is the strength of unity! God's ingenuity in the beginning divided one flesh into two; but God wanted to show that it remained one even after its division, so God made it impossible for either half to procreate without the other. Now do you see how great a mystery marriage is? From one man, Adam, God made Eve and then reunited these two into one, so that their children would be produced from a single source. Likewise, husband and wife are not two, but one.

John Chrysostom
Fourth century

WHILE it is alive
Until Death touches it
While it and I lap one Air
Dwell in one Blood
Under one Sacrament
Show me Division can split or pare —

Love is like Life — merely longer
Love is like Death, during the Grave
Love is the Fellow of the Resurrection
Scooping up the Dust and chanting "Live"!

Emily Dickinson
Nineteenth century

So they loved, as love in twain
Had the essence but in one;
Two distincts, division none:
Number there in love was slain.

Hearts remote, yet not asunder;
Distance, and no space was seen
'Twixt this turtle and his queen:
But in them it were a wonder.

So between them love did shine,
That the turtle saw his right

Flaming in the phoenix' sight;
Either was the other's mine.

Property was thus appalléd,
That the self was not the same;
Single nature's double name
Neither two nor one was calléd.

William Shakespeare
Sixteenth century

THE candle had two ends for lighting. One length had carved gold characters with Tyan-yu's name, the other mine. The matchmaker lighted both ends and announced, "The marriage has begun." Tyan yanked the scarf off my face and smiled at his friends and family, never even looking at me. He reminded me of a young peacock I once saw that acted as if he had just claimed the entire courtyard by fanning his still-short tail.

I saw the matchmaker place the lighted red candle in a gold holder and then hand it to a nervous-looking servant. This servant was supposed to watch the candle during the banquet and all night to make sure neither end went out. In the morning the matchmaker was supposed to show the result, a little piece of black ash, and then declare, "This candle burned continuously at both ends without going out. This is a marriage that can never be broken."

I still can remember. That candle was a marriage bond that was worth more than a Catholic promise not to divorce. It meant I couldn't divorce and I couldn't ever remarry, even if Tyan-yu died. That red candle was supposed to seal me forever with my husband and his family, no excuses afterward.

Amy Tan

L ET us build here an exquisite friendship,
The flame, the autumn, and the green rose of love
Fought out their strife here, 'tis a place of wonder;
Where these have been, meet 'tis, the ground is holy.

Ezra Pound

B LESS them in their work
and in their companionship;
in their sleeping and their waking;
in their joys and in their sorrows;
in their life and in their death.

An ecumenical
marriage rite

Roman liturgy    MAY they together rejoice in your gift of married love.

MY beloved speaks and says to me:
  "Arise, my love, my fair one,
  and come away;
O my dove, in the clefts of the rock,
  in the covert of the cliff,
let me see your face,
  let me hear your voice;
for your voice is sweet,
  and your face is lovely."

Song of Songs 2:10,
14, 16a    My beloved is mine and I am his.

John 15:9–11    AS the Father has loved me, so I have loved you;
abide in my love.

LADY, Lady, I saw your face,
Dark as night withholding a star . . .
The chisel fell, or it might have been
You had borne so long the yoke of men.

Lady, Lady, I saw your hands,
Twisted, awry, like crumpled roots,
Bleached poor white in a sudsy tub,
Wrinkled and drawn from your rub-a-dub.

Lady, Lady, I saw your heart,
And altared there in its darksome place
Were the tongues of flame the ancients knew,
Anne Spencer    Where the good God sits to spangle through.

A T the stars you gaze, you my bright star.
O, if I were but the sky, to hold you.
In broad embraces, and with a myriad of eyes
To feast upon you in wordless radiance.

Plato
Fourth century BCE

S HE couldn't make him look just like any other man to her. He looked like the love thoughts of women. He could be a bee to a blossom — a pear tree blossom in the spring. He seemed to be crushing scent out of the world with his footsteps. Crushing aromatic herbs with every step he took. Spices hung about him. He was a glance from God.

Zora Neale Hurston

B ECAUSE marriage is about the way couples share in the love of God, every marriage is the same and yet every marriage is different.

Kenneth W. Stevenson

L YDIA looked from one to the other of them — the terms of their argument were very familiar and they didn't worry her disproportionately. Often the sound of her parents' voices in this mode (a shade irritable, carefully, not viciously, mocking, ultimately like a single voice trying both parts impartially) was almost soothing. Children will adapt to anything as long as it holds no shock or hard surprises. And in this case it assured her that both of them were home here with her, working something out. It was only their way.

Rosellen Brown

B LESSED is the creation of joy and celebration, lover and mate, gladness and jubilation, pleasure and delight, love and solidarity, friendship and peace. Soon may we hear in the streets of the city and the paths of the fields, the voice of joy, the voice of gladness, the voice of lover, the voice of mate, the triumphant voice of lovers from the canopy and the voice of youths from their feasts of song. Blessed Blessed Blessed is the joy of lovers, one with each other.

Linda Hirschhorn and
David Cooper

H APPY is the husband of a good wife;
the number of his days will be doubled.
A loyal wife brings joy to her husband,
and he will complete his years in peace.
A good wife is a great blessing;
she will be granted among the blessings of the man
who fears the Lord.
Whether rich or poor, his heart is content,
and at all times his face is cheerful.

Sirach 26:1 – 4

T HE virtues of a good wife, so eloquently proclaimed by
Sirach, are a blessing for the husband, but at the same
time they offer him a challenge that will test his true man-
hood. They challenge him to see to it that, just as she makes
his heart content, "a smile is ever on his face," so he strives
to make a smile be ever on her face. As he is most willing
that she be thoughtful and governed in her speech, so he is
challenged to be temperate in his speech and behavior
toward her.

Robert Crotty and
John Barry Ryan

O F fair girls the loveliest
Was to meet me at the corner of the Wall.
But she hides and will not show herself;
I scratch my head, pace up and down.

Of fair girls the prettiest
Gave me a red flute.
The flush of that red flute
Is pleasure at the girl's beauty.

She has been in the pastures and brought for me
rush-wool,
Very beautiful and rare.
It is not you that are beautiful;
But you were given by a lovely girl.

Chou song
Seventh century BCE

LOVE breaks through hidden depths, its arrival fulfills and perfects, but it does not exhaust the mystery. One is loved for what one is, which allows one to accept oneself and to receive one's own being as a gift.

Paul Evdokimov

THE perfect loveliness that God has made
Wild violets shy and Heaven-mounting dreams.
And now — unwittingly, you've made me dream
Of violets, and my soul's forgotten gleam.

Alice Dunbar-Nelson

ONE has to go from a consciousness of oneself to a willingness to be oneself. When that willingness is there, one steps into oneself, into the mirror image of oneself that has been blocking one's view, and one becomes able to see the universe, to commune with all things.

John S. Dunne

I love you for your brownness,
And the rounded darkness of your breast,
I love you for the breaking sadness in your voice
And shadows where your wayward eyelids rest.

Something of the old forgotten queens
Lurks in the lithe abandon of your walk
And something of the shackled slave
Sobs in the rhythm of your talk.

Oh, little brown girl, born for sorrow's mate,
Keep all you have of queenliness,
Forgetting that you once were a slave,
And let your full lips laugh at Fate!

Gwendolyn B. Bennett

GOD keeps a loving eye
on all who believe,
on those who count on God
to bring relief from famine,
to rescue them from death.

With all we are, we wait for God,
the Lord, our help, our shield.
Our hearts find joy in the Lord;
we trust God's holy name.
Love us, Lord!

Psalm 33:18 – 22     We wait for you.

Ephrem Syrus     OLord, inflame these lovers with the fire of love; in the
Fourth century      morning of all your days, may you awake unto joy!

TWO spirits unite to face together the difficulties and the
tragedy of life. Two worlds pool their wealth and their
poverty, their history and their eternity. It is the history of
humanity beginning with Adam and Eve that is projected
into their frail existence. It is the totality of the Masculine
and the totality of the Feminine that preside over this birth
in love; in this summary of the universal they hope to detect
one reply to their expectation, a miracle. This is why every
love is always unique, and its promise is like the first sun on
Paul Evdokimov     the first morning.

SHINE forth, shine forth, O groom,
together with your true spouse,
who dwells in the habitation prepared for her.
Receive the joy and the gift of God.
It is Christ our God who gives them to you.
Go forward with joy to your nuptial chamber,
a chamber bedecked with decorations of every kind.    Coptic liturgy

BLESS these rings which we hold that they may be for
the confirmation of betrothal to those who receive them
for loving unity, for excellent and laudable manners, and
for modest and chaste matrimony. Let them, by means of
these, be shining and adorned, and be walking in the paths
that are pleasing to your Godhead. May they, with joy and
delight, attain the present bridal chamber, be worthy of the
eternal chamber of gladness, and offer praise to you, and
to your blessed Father, and to your Holy Spirit now and
evermore.    Syrian Orthodox liturgy

NOW you will feel no rain, for each of you
will be shelter to the other.
Now you will feel no cold, for each of you
will be warmth to the other.
Now there is no loneliness for you;
Now you are two persons, but there is only
one life before you;

Go now to your dwelling place to enter into
the days of your togetherness,
And may your days be good, and long together.    Apache prayer

O Lord,
those things which are blessed
by invocation of your name
are sustained by the fulness of your blessing.
Bless this room, set aside for honest marriage,
that no onslaught of evil might touch it.
May the chastity of marriage alone reign here
and may your compassion
*Liber Ordinum*    attend its worthy celebration.

MORAL theologians have said too much about the value
of virginity and about the sinfulness of the flesh, and
Catharine P. Roth    too little about the possibility of a transfigured human love.

WILD Nights — Wild Nights!
Were I with thee
Wild Nights should be
Our luxury!

Futile — the Winds —
To a Heart in port —
Done with the Compass —
Done with the Chart!

Rowing in Eden —
Ah, the Sea!
Emily Dickinson    Might I but moor — Tonight —
Nineteenth century    In Thee

LET your blessing so flow
upon their hearts and bodies
that they might feel the touch of your hand
and, by the Holy Spirit,
*Liber Ordinum*    be made sharers in everlasting happiness.

L ET my beloved come into his garden" (Song of Songs 4:16). The Torah teaches gentle manners: The bridegroom should not enter the marriage-chamber until the bride gives him leave.

Pesikta Rabbati
Rabbinic literature

M ARRIAGE could catch on again because living together is not quite living and not quite together.

Gerald Nachman

M ARRIAGE in Christian reality is, by contrast, a roaring lion with strength and vigor and health and dignity that challenge faithful and faithless alike to reach out for a better way of living together under the shadow of the King of Kings and Lord of Lords.

Marriage is ultimately about our doctrine of God, no less. It is about the way we celebrate God's very heart and existence, his love stretching out to us as we enjoy each other's company and go so far as to procreate successive generations who may become God's people on earth, where he reigns in glory and vulnerability.

Kenneth W. Stevenson

H USBANDS, love your wives, just as Christ loved the church and gave himself up for her, in order to make her holy by cleansing her with the washing of water by the word, so as to present the church to himself in splendor, without a spot or wrinkle or anything of the kind — yes, so that she may be holy and without blemish. In the same way, husbands should love their wives as they do their own bodies. He who loves his wife loves himself. For no one ever hates his own body, but he nourishes and tenderly cares for it, just as Christ does for the church, because we are members of his body. "For this reason a man will leave his father and mother and be joined to his wife, and the two will become one flesh." This is a great mystery, and I am applying it to Christ and the church. Each of you, however, should love his wife as himself, and a wife should respect her husband.

Ephesians 5:25 – 33

HUSBANDS, love your wives . . . and a wife should respect her husband"; notice Paul's choice of words. In this passage, there is no mention of greater or lesser authority. Why does he speak here in terms of equality? Because his subject is conjugal fidelity. He intends for the husband to have the greater responsibility in nearly every concern, but fidelity is an exception: "The husband does not rule over his own body, but the wife does." Husband and wife are equally responsible for the honor of their marriage bed.

*John Chrysostom*
*Fourth century*

FATHER, creator of the world,
you gave life to every living creature
and commissioned human beings to multiply.
With your own hands, you gave Adam a companion:
bones grown from his bones,
to signify identity of form
yet wondrous diversity.
Thus your command to share the marriage bed,
to increase and multiply in marriage,
has lined the whole world together
and established ties among the whole human race.
This you saw, O Lord, to be pleasing, even necessary:
they who were previously two become one;
while from that oneness of love both sexes derive.

*Leonine Sacramentary*

LET all thy joys be as the month of May,
And all thy days be as a marriage day:
Let sorrow, sickness, and a troubled mind
Be stranger to thee, let them never find
Thy heart at home.

*Frances Quarles*
*Seventeenth century*

FTER all, the rosy love-making and marrying and Epithalamy are no more than the dawn of things, and to follow comes all the spacious interval of white laborious light. Try as we may to stay those delightful moments they fade and pass remorselessly; there is no returning, no recovering, only — for the foolish — the vilest peep-shows and imitations in dens and darkened rooms. We go on — we grow. At least we age. Our young couple, emerging presently from an atmosphere of dusk and morning stars, found the sky gathering grayly overhead and saw one another for the first time clearly in the light of every day.    H. G. Wells

T was frightening, the trees in their rigid postures
using up the sun,
as the earth tilted its essential degree.
Snow covered everything. Its confusing glare
doubled the view
so that I saw you approach
my empty house
not as one man, but as a landscape
repeating along the walls of every room
papering over the cracked grief.

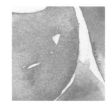

I knew as I stepped into the design,
as I joined the chain of hands,
and let the steeple of fire
be raised above our heads.
We had chosen the costliest pattern,

the strangest, the most enduring.
We were afraid as we stood between the willows,
as we shaped the standard words with our tongues.
Then it was done. The scenery multiplied
around us and we turned.
We stared calmly from the pictures.    Louise Erdrich

O make these loved companions greatly to rejoice,
even as of old you gladdened your creature
in the garden of Eden.
Blessed are you, O Lord,
who makes bridegroom and bride to rejoice.

*Jewish liturgy*

THE brandisht Sword of God before them blaz'd
Fierce as a Comet; which with torrid heat,
And vapour as the *Libyan* Air adust,
Began to parch that temperat Clime; whereat
In either hand the hastning Angel caught
Our lingring Parents, and to th' Eastern Gate
Led them direct, and down the Cliff as fast
To the subjected Plain; then disappear'd.
They looking back, all th' Eastern side beheld
Of Paradise, so late thir happie seat,
Wav'd over by that flaming Brand, the Gate
With dreadful Faces throngd and fierie Arms:
Som natural tears they dropd, but wip'd them soon;
The World was all before them, where to choose
Thir place of rest, and Providence thir guide:
They hand in hand with wandring steps and slow,
Through *Eden* took their solitarie way.

*John Milton*
*Seventeenth century*

MARRIAGE is given that husband and wife may comfort
and help each other, living faithfully together in deed
and in plenty, in sorrow and in joy. It is given, that with
delight and tenderness that they might know each other in
love, and, through the joy of their bodily union, may
strengthen the union of their hearts and lives. It is given,
that they may have children and be blessed in caring for
them and bringing them up in accordance with God's will,
to his praise and glory.

*The Alternative Service*
*Book*
*Church of England*

TEVYE:

D<small>O</small> you love me?

GOLDE:

Do I love him?
For twenty-five years I've lived with him,
Fought with him, starved with him.
Twenty-five years my bed is his.
If that's not love, what is!

TEVYE:

Then do you love me?

GOLDE:

I suppose I do.

TEVYE:

And I suppose I love you, too.

TEVYE AND GOLDE:

It doesn't change a thing,
But even so,
After twenty-five years,
It's nice to know.

Sheldon Harnick

T<small>HEN</small> they were lovers, finally. Finally in love; or near love. Then one would advance a little too precipitously and the other would instinctively withdraw, and when the first one, relenting, would return, the other would have soberly reconsidered; and this was love.

Joyce Carol Oates

I<small>N</small> expressing love we belong among the undeveloped countries.

Saul Bellow

Sarum Breviary

MOST merciful God, the helper of all, so strengthen us by thy power, that our sorrows may be turned into joy, and we may continually glorify thy holy name; through Jesus Christ our Lord.

Paul Evdokimov

LOVE does not depend on the "order of the day," but on the order of the last day.

Roman liturgy

BELOVED of Christ: The union of man and woman in Christian marriage is brought about by God and for the purposes of God. The prompting to enter this holy state has come, we trust, from God, rather than from any mere passing affection on your part. In the sacred contract which you are about to ratify, God is ever a third partner, and as you plight yourselves to each other, you are giving yourselves over to the fulfilment of God's plans. All the while God stands by to accompany your union with the assistance of divine grace, so that you may thankfully accept its blessings and faithfully fulfil its duties.

John Chrysostom
Fourth century

TWO souls so united have nothing to fear. With harmony, peace and mutual love, man and woman own all possessions. They can live in peace behind the impregnable wall that protects them, which is love according to God. By love's grace, they are harder than diamond and stronger than iron, they sail in abundance, steer a course toward eternal glory and attract more and more grace from God.

B ECAUSE you come to me with naught but love,
and hold my hand and lift mine eyes above,
a wider world of hope and joy I see,
because you come to me.

Because God made thee mine, I'll cherish thee
through light and darkness for all time to be,
and pray his love may make our love divine,
because God made thee mine.                                    Edward Teschemacher

G RANT them, Lord,
to live faithfully in the companionship of love.
May they be endowed with the charity of Sarah,
the wisdom of Rebecca,
the love of Rachel,
and the grace and charity of Susanna.
May it descend upon these your servants,
as the gentle rain falls upon the face of the earth.
May they feel the action of your hand,
and your Holy Spirit,
and attain to everlasting joy.                                    *Bobbio Missal*

M AY the halo of pray'r
And the mantle of peace
As heav'n's benediction descend,
Ordaining our lives
for the mission of Christ,
And love with our sacrifice blend.                                    Shaker hymn

THEREFORE the sacred partnership of true marriage is constituted both by the will of God and the will of human beings. From God comes the very institution of marriage, the ends for which it was instituted, the laws that govern it, the blessings that flow from it; while an individual, through generous surrender of his or her own person made to another for the whole span of life, becomes, with the help and cooperation of God, the author of each particular marriage, with the duties and blessings annexed thereto from divine institution.

Pius XI

So — in the self-forgetfulness of concentrated
    attention —
  the door opens for you into a pure living intimacy,
A shared, timeless happiness,
Conveyed by a smile,
A wave of the hand.

Dag Hammarskjöld

MANY times a day Abraham would take Ann in his arms and hug her and kiss her and tell her he loved her. If he left the house for even a few minutes he would kiss her and tell her he loved her. He didn't need to tell her. She knew that he loved her. But the telling was a pleasure. And every day, also, he told her she was beautiful, and when he did she would go and sit in his lap and he would kiss her and tell her he loved her, and she told him she loved him again and again, for her love for him was always welling up and overflowing, and it was a pleasure to be able always to tell him, without embarrassment, how she loved him, without restraint, she loved him, without fear that her love wouldn't be returned. It *was* returned, over and over, and she never got tired of hearing it.

Sherril Jaffe

W HEN Christians marry they are expected to bring to the marriage a sense of transformation that makes their love for one another a sign of the love of God for us made visible in Jesus. Thus, both the Church wedding and the wedding reception in their own ways proclaim, "Let us love one another totally, let us see that all present are satisfied, and let each one respond joyfully to the love made visible in the couple."

Robert Crotty and
John Barry Ryan

T HIS is my commandment, that you love one another as I have loved you. No one has greater love than this, to lay down one's life for one's friends. You are my friends if you do what I command you. I do not call you servants any longer, because the servant does not know what the master is doing; but I have called you friends, because I have made known to you everything that I have heard from my Father. You did not choose me but I choose you. And I appointed you to go and bear fruit, fruit that will last, so that the Father will give you whatever you ask him in my name.

John 15:12–16

*Book of Common
Prayer*

GIVE them wisdom and devotion in the ordering of their common life, that each may be to the other a strength in need, a counselor in perplexity, a comfort in sorrow, and a companion in joy.

1 Corinthians 13:4 – 8a

Love is patient; love is kind; love is not envious or boastful or arrogant or rude. It does not insist on its own way; it is not irritable or resentful; it does not rejoice in wrongdoing, but rejoices in the truth. It bears all things, believes all things, hopes all things, endures all things. Love never ends.

Robert Crotty and John
Barry Ryan

IF, as Paul has it, real love never fails, it is because it is not self-seeking. It lives and works not for itself, but for the loved one. If a marriage is to endure in the midst of the problems that inevitably beset it, it is only because the two people are truly united. They realize that marriage is not mere existence — I won't bother you if you don't bother me. It means that I will actually be good and kind and loving to you, no matter what the cost.

Genesis Rabbah

RABBI Jacob said: He who has no wife lives without good, or help, or joy, or blessing, or atonement. Rabbi Joshua of Sikhnin, in the name of Rabbi Levi, added that he is also without life. Rabbi Miyya ben Gammada said that he is not really a complete man, and some say that he diminishes the divine likeness.

THESE are the virtues Calvin thought desirable
In a wife: an even mood,
Chastity, patience, thrift, and an untirable
Solicitude

For her lord's health. Here ends the simple list—
And not one word
Tells us if he admired a delicate wrist
Or much preferred
A hazel eye to brown or amethyst.
What! Had he not some choice
Of statures? Was he not partial in the matter
Of a right female voice,
Desire but silence or a wrenlike chatter?
And did not kindness count, or a cool repose?
A cheek of white-and-rose?
Or courtesy? Or wit?

All very well that it should not obtain
If she were fair or plain
(Since by philosophy one must admit,
In this connection,
A woman's flesh is but the spirit's mask)

But ah! not even to ask
That in her breast some taper of affection,
Some flame however decorous and dim
Should burn, and burn especially for him.

Of Mistress Calvin we know little save
She was eight years a wife,
Well-dowered, also "honorable and grave"
And lived a quiet life.
One hopes against hope that she was debonair
And managed to mingle with connubial care
For his dyspepsia, some small tendernesses.
But miracles are rare.
One's better guess is
(And all we have is Calvin's list to go on)
That since he asked, beside a sensible dot
Only thrift, patience, chastity and so on,
Likely it's what he got.                    Phyllis McGinley

S HE knew that nothing would get better, that it would never be any different. He had lost interest in his work, and no longer did anything. Because, he said, he was not given a free hand. And now she was sitting there praying for his freedom, praying because she so wanted to believe that he was being unfairly treated, that, if only he was given his freedom, he would become a man again. Wanted to believe it so that she might keep up her belief in him. She knew what the true answer was, but she had to force herself to listen to it: he was as free as anybody can be in the economic mazes of a modern society, and any external change would only bring him fresh disappointment. The situation would repeat itself, and he would discover that everything was just as it had been before.

Yes, yes — And she knew more: knew that there could never be a way out. Because behind all his talk of freedom lay hidden a child's wish to conquer death, a lack of interest in any piece of work the result of which would not be *his,* even long after he was dead. — And yet she sat there praying.

Dag Hammarskjöld

W HAT would you raise next year on that land we cleared of brush down by the creek? The hay on it is too thin, and it must be broken up." This was the question for my consideration at the breakfast table, and my answer was, "Raise the same crop on that as you do on the remainder of the land on that side of the creek. One large field is better than two small ones, and time is saved in working. Put it into the regular rotation with the rest."

Not that the Man of the Place would do as I said unless he agreed with me, but getting my ideas helps him to form his own opinions, and he knows that two heads are better at planning than one.

Laura Ingalls Wilder

Y OU, my friend, are lonely because...
   With pointing words and fingers
we slowly make the world our
own, perhaps its weakest, most precarious

part. Who points a finger at a smell?
But you feel many of the powers
that threaten us . . . You know the dead,
and you cower from the magic spell.

See, now we must bear the pieces and parts
together, as if they were the whole.
Helping you will be hard. Above all,

don't plant me in your heart. I'd grow too fast.
But I shall guide my master's hand and say:
Here. This is Esau in his pelt.                      Rainer Maria Rilke

I wouldn't coax the plant if I were you.
  Such watchful nurturing may do it harm.
Let the soil rest from so much digging
And wait until it's dry before you water it.
The leaf's inclined to find its own direction;
Give it a chance to seek the sunlight for itself.

Much growth is stunted by too careful prodding,
Too eager tenderness.
The things we love we have to learn to leave alone.        Naomi Long Madgett

P EOPLE become lovers because they are persistent in getting to know one another, and couples deepen their
love only through the persistent effort of responding to one        Robert Crotty and
another daily.                                                      John Barry Ryan

IT'S not talk of God and the decade ahead that
Allows you to get through the worst.
It's "I do" and "You don't" and "Nobody said that"
And "Who brought the subject up first?"
It's the little things, the little things, the little
     things . . .
It's the little things, the little things, the little
     things . . .
The little ways you try together,
Cry together,
Lie together,
That make perfect relationships,
Becoming a cliché together,
Growing old and gray together.

Steven Sondheim

ONE reason that many couples have written private,
rather than legally binding, marriage contracts is that
they have found they have had to change and reinterpret
many agreements as they went on in their married life. The
important thing, most people have said, is that they spent
the time *beforehand* to try to figure out what their problems
might be after the euphoria of the honeymoon was over. In
the process of talking out their questions, they dealt with
many problems and issues they didn't even know were
there. Again, it is the process, not the plan itself, that made
the difference.

Howard Kirschenbaum
and Rockwell Stensrud

WHILE we acknowledge our mutual affection by pub-
licly assuming the relationship of husband and wife
. . . we deem it a duty to declare that this act on our part
implies no sanction of, nor promise of, voluntary obedience
to such of the present laws of marriage as refuse to recognize
the wife as an independent, rational being, while they con-
fer upon the husband an injurious and unnatural superiority.

Lucy Stone
Nineteenth century

B E subject to one another out of reverence for Christ.      Ephesians 5:21

T HE lover desires the perfection of the beloved — which requires, among other things, the liberation of the beloved from the lover.      Dag Hammarskjöld

I N all unions, one receives the other, and both receive from each other.      Judah Loew ben Bezalel
Sixteenth century

C AROLINE Braxley, this capable and handsome bride-to-be of mine, was a very remarkable girl, just as today, as my wife, she seems to be a very remarkable woman of sixty. She and I have been married for forty-one years now, and her good judgment in all matters relating to our marriage has never failed her — or us. She had already said to me before that Saturday afternoon that a successful marriage depended in part on the two persons' developing and maintaining a certain number of separate interests in life. She was all for my keeping up my golf, my hunting, my fishing. And, unlike my own family, she saw no reason that I shouldn't keep up my peculiar interest in Latin, though she had to confess that she thought it almost the funniest thing she had ever heard of a man of my sort going in for.      Peter Taylor

T HERE may be fewer divorces in the country without its necessarily following that there are more happy homes. It seems to me that the deadly monotony of working with, and playing with, the same person in the same place for days and weeks and months and years would be more apt to drive a person to divorce or suicide than if they were separated during the working day and could meet when it was over, with different experiences to talk about and to add variety to their companionship.      Laura Ingalls Wilder

John S. Dunne

THE way of necessity and the way of possibility turn out to be one and the same way.

WE are
ready for the night
have done the final
chores spoken of the
earlier rap emptied
ashtrays cleared the notes
and records from the
floor. Tiredness pulls
at my legs heavies
my hands as I wash
my face then shrug off
the robe. I bump the
bed in darkness and
fumble at the sheets.

Asleep you reach for me your body
curves around mine. You breathe even and
quiet now and briefly touch my breast my hip. I
believe you know it is my hand you
hold know my neck beneath your
lip.
And I am
satisfied:
You love me.

Sherley Anne Williams

MAY the words and actions of those who enter here
to celebrate their marriage be so proper
that they are never swept away by desire

Liber Ordinum    to the shipwreck of passion.

I want to write you
a love poem as headlong
as our creek
after thaw
when we stand
on its dangerous
banks and watch it carry
with it every twig
every dry leaf and branch
in its path
every scruple
when we see it
so swollen
with runoff
that even as we watch
we must grab
each other
and step back
we must grab each
other or
get our shoes
soaked we must
grab each other

Linda Pastan

EVERY man who is high up loves to think that he has done
it all himself; and the wife smiles, and lets it go at that.

James Matthew Barrie
Nineteenth century

YOUR love must be one that goes deeper than
good looks.
Christ has made up to you by endowing your soul
with riches that endure.
Both of you he has enriched with holy wedding gifts:
hope, devotion, fidelity, peace, and chastity.
God's word is your silver,
your gold the Holy Spirit;
the jewels you possess are the brightness of good works
glowing in your hearts.

Paulinus of Nola
Fourth century

LOVE is a kindling of one's mind and heart that gives one
the willingness to know and the courage to face one's
darkness.

John S. Dunne

HE saw all those private aspects of me — and I mean not
just sexual private parts, but my darker side, my mean-
ness, my pettiness, my self-loathing — all the things I kept
hidden. So that with him I was completely naked, and
when I was feeling the most vulnerable — when the wrong
word would have sent me flying out the door forever — he
always said exactly the right thing at the right moment. He
didn't allow me to cover myself up. He would grab my
hands, look me straight in the eye and tell me something
new about why he loved me.

Amy Tan

MARRIAGE is ambiguous, it is "assiduous supposing." It is thus not only celebration, joy and making merry, but marriage has its hidden and darker sides. These include the life being left behind, the covering of nudity with special clothes, and fear of the future. Sometimes these realities are expressed most dramatically in movies, where reality can be coped with because it is presented in a stylized form. All three of the darker features just mentioned are the reverse side of a coin. The life being left behind leads into a life together in the future. The covering of nudity leads into the ecstasy of sexual intercourse (although here, again, there is a mystery because sexual life does not always start at marriage, nor is it necessarily "successful" and fulfilling until later). Finally, fear of the future leads into the fact that the couple at least will have each other without social or familial constraints, or at least a reduction of them. The very fact that these contrasts have had to be qualified serves to show that marriage is not meant just to be "happy." It involves pain of all kinds, it brings opportunities for growth, it is not just "honey."

Kenneth W. Stevenson

ALTHOUGH you are sovereign in strength, you judge with mildness,
and with great forbearance you govern us;
for you have power to act whenever you choose.

Through such works you have taught your people
that the righteous must be kind,
and you have filled your children with good hope,
because you give repentance for sins.

Wisdom 12:18 – 19

WHEN St. Macarius, the great ascetic, lived in the desert, an angel appeared to him, ordering that he follow him to a remote town. Upon arriving there, he made him enter a poor dwelling where a humble family lived. The angel showed him the wife and mother of this household and told him that she had become a saint by living in peace and perfect harmony with all her family, since her marriage, in the midst of daily occupations, keeping a chaste heart, a deep humility, and a burning love for God. And St. Macarius entreated God for the grace to live in the desert as this woman had lived in the world.

Paul Evdokimov

IN all the Eastern rites, and in some of the Western rites, marriage is celebrated as a passage from one form of life to another.

Kenneth W. Stevenson

WHILE my hair was still cut straight across my forehead
I played about the front gate, pulling flowers.
You came by on bamboo stilts, playing horse,
You walked about my seat, playing with blue plums.
And we went on living in the village of Chokan:
Two small people, without dislike or suspicion.

At fourteen I married My Lord you.
I never laughed, being bashful.
Lowering my head, I looked at the wall.
Called to, a thousand times, I never looked back.

At fifteen I stopped scowling,
I desired my dust to be mingled with yours
For ever and for ever and for ever.
Why should I climb the look out?

At sixteen you departed,
You went into far Ku-to-yen, by the river of the
    swirling eddies,
And you have been gone five months.
The monkeys make sorrowful noise overhead.

You dragged your feet when you went out.
By the gate now, the moss is grown, the different mosses,
Too deep to clear them away!
The leaves fall early this autumn, in wind.
The paired butterflies are already yellow with August
Over the grass in the West garden;
They hurt me. I grow older.
If you are coming down through the narrows
    of the river Kiang,
Please let me know beforehand,
And I will come out to meet you
                            As far as Cho-fu-Sa.                    Ezra Pound


Low much the wife is dearer than the bride.     George Lyttelton
                                                 Eighteenth century


LET mutual love continue. Do not neglect to show hospitality to strangers, for by doing that some have enter-
tained angels without knowing it. Remember those who are
in prison, as though you were in prison with them; those
who are being tortured, as though you yourselves were
being tortured. Let marriage be held in honor by all, and let
the marriage bed be kept undefiled; for God will judge for-
nicators and adulterers. Keep your lives free from the love
of money, and be content with what you have; for he has
said, "I will never leave you or forsake you." So we can say
with confidence,

"The Lord is my helper;
    I will not be afraid.
What can anyone do to me?"                       Hebrews 13:1 – 6

LEARNING to love differently is hard,
love with the hands wide open, love
with the doors banging on their hinges,
the cupboard unlocked, the wind
roaring and whimpering in the rooms
rustling the sheets and snapping the blinds
that thwack like rubber bands
in an open palm.

It hurts to love wide open
stretching the muscles that feel
as if they are made of wet plaster,
then of blunt knives, then
of sharp knives.

It hurts to thwart the reflexes
of grab, of clutch; to love and let
go again and again. It pesters to remember
the lover who is not in the bed,
to hold back what is owed to the work
that gutters like a candle in a cave
without air, to love consciously,
conscientiously, concretely, constructively.

I can't do it, you say it's killing
me, but you thrive, you glow
on the street like a neon raspberry,
You float and sail, a helium balloon
bright bachelor's button blue and bobbing
on the cold and hot winds of our breath,
as we make and unmake in passionate
diastole and systole the rhythm
of our unbound bonding, to have
and not to hold, to love
with minimized malice, hunger
Marge Piercy    and anger moment by moment balanced.

I ask but one thing of you, only one,
   That always you will be my dream of you;
   That never shall I wake to find untrue
All this I have believed and rested on,
Forever vanished, like a vision gone
   Out into the night. Alas, how few
   There are who strike in us a chord we knew
Existed, but so seldom heard its tone
   We tremble at the half-forgotten sound.
The world is full of rude awakenings
   And heaven-born castles shattered to the ground,
Yet still our human longing vainly clings
   To a belief in beauty through all wrongs.
   O stay your hand, and leave my heart its songs!

                                        Amy Lowell

AH, love, let us be true
   To one another! for the world, which seems
To lie before us like a land of dreams,
So various, so beautiful, so new,
Hath really neither joy, nor love, nor light,
Nor certitude, nor peace, nor help for pain;
And we are here as on a darkling plain
Swept with confused alarms of struggle and flight,    Matthew Arnold
Where ignorant armies clash by night.                 Nineteenth century

IF God does not build the house,
the builders work in vain.
                                        Psalm 127:1

Mᴀʏ they both praise you when they are happy and
turn to you in their sorrows.

Roman liturgy

Yᴏᴜ have made the Lord as refuge,
you have made the Most High your stronghold.

No evil shall ever touch you,
no harm come near your home.
God instructs angels
to guard you wherever you go.

With their hands they support you,
so your foot will not strike a stone.
You will tread on lion and viper,
trample tawny lion and dragon.

"I deliver all who cling to me,
raise the ones who know me,
answer those who call me,
stand with those in trouble.
These I rescue and honor,
satisfy with long life,
and show my power to save."

Psalm 91:9–16

Nᴏ time like today for thine own,
Today for thy cross and thy crown;
today may victories won
Establish thy feet in God's way.
Today tho' the vintage may fail,
And answer to prayer seem to wait,
Still let thy faith cheer thee today,
God's blessings can never be late.

Shaker hymn

KEEP us, Lord, so awake in the duties of our calling that we may sleep in thy peace and wake in thy glory.

John Donne
Seventeenth century

WE are not excused from our duties by our spouse's delinquency. A wife must still respect an unloving husband; a husband must still love a disrespectful wife.

Catharine P. Roth

LORD give us grace
that we may know that in the darkness pressing round
it is the mist of sin that hides thy face
that thou art there
and thou dost know we love thee still.

Gilbert Shaw

DEAR God, it is so very hard for us not to be anxious,
we worry about work and money,
about food and health,
about weather and crops,
about war and politics,
about loving and being loved.
Show us how perfect love casts out fear.

Monica Furlong

MAY the one who sent the archangel Raphael
to prepare the marriage of Tobias and Sarah
send holy angels from the heavenly throne
to comfort you in holy service,
show you the path of righteousness
and protect you for ever from all evil.

Benedictional of
Robert of Jumieges

TRUST God and do good,
settle down and be at peace.
Delight in the Lord
who satisfies your heart.

Give your life to the Lord.
Trust God to act on your behalf,

to make your integrity shine forth
and your justice bright as noon.

Be still, wait for the Lord.
Waste no energy fretting
Psalm 37:3 – 7    about the success of evil schemers.

PRESERVE them, O Lord our God,
as you preserved the three holy children from the fire,
Byzantine liturgy    sending down upon them dew from heaven.

TURN to God, be bright with joy;
you shall never be let down.
I begged and God heard,
took my burdens from me.

God's angel defends the faithful,
guards them on every side.
Drink in the richness of God,
enjoy the strength of the Lord.

Live in awe of God, you saints:
Psalm 34:6 – 10    you will want for nothing.

BLESS us thro' all cares and burdens,
O'er the stormy sea of life;
Stay us, Lord, in our afflictions,
Help us in the glorious strife.
Tho' the way be rough and thorny,
Flowers often hidden be,
Perilous the road we travel,
We will ever trust in thee.

Shaker hymn

BLESSED are you, O Lord our God,
king of the universe,
who has created joy and gladness,
bridegroom and bride,
mirth and exultation,
pleasure and delight,
love, peace and fellowship.
Soon may there be heard in the cities of Judah,
and in the streets of Jerusalem,
the voice of joy and gladness,
the voice of the bridegroom and the voice of the bride,
the jubilant voice of the bridegrooms from their canopies,
and of youths from their feasts of song.
Blessed are you, O Lord,
who makes the bridegroom to rejoice with the bride.

Jewish liturgy

MARRIAGE resembles a pair of shears, so joined that they
can not be separated; often moving in opposite direc-
tions, yet always punishing anyone who comes between
them.

Sydney Smith
Nineteenth century

Now that I'm angry at Harold, it's hard to remember what was so remarkable about him. And I know they're there, the good qualities, because I wasn't that stupid to fall in love with him, to marry him. All I can remember is how awfully lucky I felt, and consequently how worried I was that all this undeserved good fortune would someday slip away. When I fantasized about moving in with him, I also dredged up my deepest fears: that he would tell me I smelled bad, that I had terrible bathroom habits, that my taste in music and television was appalling. I worried that Harold would someday get a new prescription for his glasses and he'd put them on one morning, look me up and down, and say, "Why, gosh, you aren't the girl I thought you were, are you?"

Amy Tan

Marriage is the hell of false expectations, where both partners, expecting to be loved, defined and supported, abdicate responsibility for themselves and accuse the other of taking away freedom.

Kathrin Perutz

We constantly overestimate the existing content of consciousness, and it is a great and surprising discovery when we find that what we had supposed to be the final peak is nothing but the first step in a very long climb. The greater the area of unconsciousness, the less is marriage a matter of free choice, as is shown subjectively in the fatal compulsion one feels so acutely when one is in love.

Carl Jung

Love gilds us over and makes us show fine things to one another for a time, but soon the gold wears off and then again the native brass appears.

George Etherege
Seventeenth century

THUS grief still treads upon the heels of pleasure;
Married in haste, we may repent at leisure.

William Congreve
Seventeenth century

NOTHING anybody tells you about marriage helps.

Max Siegel

SELDOM or never does a marriage develop into an individual relationship smoothly and without crises. There is no birth of consciousness without pain.

Carl Jung

IT is the *huppah* [wedding canopy] that we take for our home when we are promising each other everything. It is raised, for most of us, once in a lifetime. It is not permanent. But it is the promise of a home.

Its openness pledges that there will be no secrets. Friends and family stand at the corners, weighing the fragile structure down. The roof is often a *tallit* [prayer shawl] so that the bride and groom are covered by holiness and the memory of commandments.

The *huppah* does not promise that love or hope or pledges will keep out weather or catastrophe. But its few lines are a sketch for what might be.

The man and woman have left the desert of their loneliness. They have come from far away to be together. The flimsiness of the *huppah* reminds them that the only thing that is real about a home is the people in it who love and choose to be together, to be a family. The only anchor that they will have will be holding onto each others' hands.

The *huppah* is the house of promises. It is the home of hope.

Debra Cash

S HOW him how happy a thing can be, how innocent
     and ours;
how even grief's lament purely determines its own shape,
serves as a thing, or dies in a thing — and escapes
in ecstasy beyond the violin. And these things, whose lives
are lived in leaving — they understand
          when you praise them.
Perishing, they turn to us, the most perishable, for help.
They want us to change them completely
          in our invisible hearts,
*Rainer Maria Rilke*   oh — forever — into us! Whoever we finally may be.

O UR God is good, give thanks!
     God is lasting love!
Our God of gods, give thanks!
God is lasting love!
Our Lord of lords, give thanks!
*Psalm 136:1 – 3*   God is lasting love!

B LESSED be our God in whose abode is joy
     and of whose bounty we have partaken
*Jewish liturgy*   and through whose goodness we live.

S ET me as a seal upon your heart,
   as a seal upon your arm;
for love is strong as death,
   passion fierce as the grave.
Its flashes are flashes of fire,
   a raging flame.
Many waters cannot quench love,
   neither can floods drown it.
If one offered for love
   all the wealth of his house,
   it would be utterly scorned.                    Song of Songs 8:6 – 7

W HO will separate us from the love of Christ? Will hardship, or distress, or persecution, or famine, or nakedness, or peril, or sword? No, in all these things we are more than conquerors through him who loved us. For I am convinced that neither death, nor life, nor angels, nor rulers, nor things present, nor things to come, nor powers, nor height, nor depth, nor anything else in all creation, will be able to separate us from the love of God in Christ Jesus our Lord.                    Roman 8:35, 37 – 39

GRANT that their wills may be so knit together in your will, and their spirits in your Spirit, that they may grow in love and peace with you and one another all the days of their life.

*Book of Common Prayer*

YOU shall love the Lord your God with all your heart, and with all your soul, and with all your mind." This is the greatest and first commandment. And a second is like it: "You shall love your neighbor as yourself." On these two commandments hang all the law and the prophets.

Matthew 22:36 – 40

THE heart can think of no devotion
Greater than being shore to the ocean —
Holding the curve of one position,
Counting an endless repetition.

Robert Frost

A blessing of matrimony is love — love in that noble sense which seeks primarily the good of the beloved, the good of the soul as well as that of the body. It was this thought which prompted St. Paul to cry out: "Husbands love your wives as Christ also loved the church."

*Roman Ritual*

I remember the devotion of your youth,
your love as a bride,
how you followed me in the wilderness,
in a land not sown.

Jeremiah 2:2

M ARY sat watching him intently, trying to find any change in his face. It is hard to see anyone who has become like your own body to you. Yes, his hair had got thin, and his high forehead had deep lines running from left to right. But his neck, always clean-shaven except in the busiest seasons, was not loose or baggy. It was burned a dark reddish brown, and there were deep creases in it, but it look firm and full of blood. His cheeks had a good color. On either side of his mouth there was a half-moon down the length of his cheek, not wrinkles, but two lines that had come there from his habitual expression. He was shorter and broader than when she married him; his back had grown broad and curved, a good deal like the shell of an old turtle, and his arms and legs were short.

He was fifteen years older than Mary, but she had hardly ever thought about it before. He was her man, and the kind of man she liked. She was rough, and he was gentle — city-bred, as she always said. They had been shipmates on a rough voyage and had stood by each other in trying times. Life had gone well with them because, at bottom, they had the same ideas about life. They agreed, without discussion, as to what was most important and what was secondary. They didn't often exchange opinions, even in Czech — it was as if they had thought the same thought together. A good deal had to be sacrificed and thrown overboard in a hard life like theirs, and they had never disagreed as to the things that could go. It had been a hard life, and a soft life, too. There wasn't anything brutal in the short, broad-backed man with the three-cornered eyes and the forehead that went on to the top of his skull. He was a city man, a gentle man, and though he had married a rough farm girl, he had never touched her without gentleness.

Willa Cather

I T was as if they had leapt over the arduous calvary of conjugal life and gone straight to the heart of love. They were together in silence like an old married couple wary of life, beyond the pitfalls of passion, beyond the brutal mockery of hope and the phantoms of disillusion: beyond love. For they had lived together long enough to know that love was always love, anytime and anyplace, but it was more solid the closer it came to death.

Gabriel García Márquez

*Gelasian Sacramentary*

MAY they be joined together in the union of marriage by mutual affection, similar minds and shared holiness.

Michael Cunningham

WE settled ourselves and lay side by side, breathing in the darkness. It seemed there should be so much for us to talk about. Perhaps the biggest surprise of married life was its continuing formality, even as you came to know the other's flesh and habits better than you knew your own. For all that familiarity, we could still seem like two people on a date that was not going particularly well.

Olivier Clement

IN the misery and disorder of our lives, true love thus demands — like monasticism, but in a more humble and apparently more prosaic way — asceticism and sanctification. Moreover, it implies, with man as with woman, an "interiorized monasticism," the healthy solitude that each must respect in the other in order to keep alive the sense of one's otherness. At times, only distance allows one to perceive the unity; only an awareness that the more the other is known the more he or she is unknown creates the deepening and the renewal of love.

Psalm 103:17 – 18

GOD's love is from all ages,
God's justice beyond all time
for believers of each generation:
those who keep the covenant,
who take care to live the law.

Paulinus of Nola
Fourth century

LET the holy cross be the yoke that pairs you together.

LEARN from this spent and slain Lamb how . . . he set himself to eating with pleasure the food of his Father's honor and our salvation at the table of the shameful cross, ignoring his own exhaustion and anguish. . . . Who is there with a heart so mean that it could look at this knight and captain who was victorious even when dead, and not rise above his or her own weakness and become courageous in the face of any adversary? No one! This is why I told you to set Christ crucified before you as the object of your contemplation.

Catherine of Siena
Fourteenth century

THAT I may come near to her, draw me nearer to thee than to her; that I may know her, make me to know thee more than her; that I may love her with the perfect love of a perfectly whole heart, cause me to love thee more than her and most of all. Amen. Amen.

That nothing may be between me and her, be thou between us, every moment. That we may be constantly together, draw us into separate loneliness with thyself. And when we meet breast to breast, my God, let it be on thine own. Amen. Amen.

Temple Gairdner
Nineteenth century

WHEN you have reached the point where you no longer expect a response, you will at last be able to give in such a way that the other is able to receive, and be grateful.

Dag Hammarskjöld

MAY God by whose will the world and all creation have their being, and who wills the life of all — may Christ, the true bridegroom, seal your marriage in the truth of his love. As he finds joy in his church, so may you find your happiness in one another; that your union may abound in love and your coming together in purity. May his angel guide you, may his peace reign between you, that in all things you may be guarded and guided, so that you may give thanks to the Father who will bless you, the Son who will rejoice in you, and the spirit who will protect you, now and for ever and world without end.

Syrian Orthodox liturgy

THERE are no successful marriages. There are only those that are succeeding — or failing.

Wells Goodrich

THE spirit of the marriage left the bedroom and took to living in the parlor. It was there to shake hands whenever company came to visit, but it never went back inside the bedroom again. So she put something in there to represent the spirit like a Virgin Mary image in a church. The bed was no longer a daisy-field for her and Joe to play in. It was a place where she went and laid down when she was sleepy and tired.

Zora Neale Hurston

M Y words are nearly always an offense.
I don't know how to speak of anything
So as to please you. But I might be taught
I should suppose. I can't say I see how.
A man must partly give up being a man
With women-folk. We could have some arrangement
By which I'd bind myself to keep hands off
Anything special you're a-mind to name.
Though I don't like such things 'twixt those that love.
Two that don't love can't live together without them.
But two that do can't live together with them."
She moved the latch a little. "Don't — don't go.
Don't carry it to someone else this time.
Tell me about it if it's something human.
Let me into your grief."

Robert Frost

T HE woman, for her part,
should seek equality with her consecrated husband
by humbly welcoming Christ's presence in her spouse. . . .
In a marriage such as this
Eve's subservience came to an end,
and Sarah became the free equal of her holy husband.
When Jesus' friends were married like this,
he attended as a groomsman,
and changed water into wine like nectar.

Paulinus of Nola
Fourth century

B Y matrimony the souls of the contracting parties are
joined and knit together more directly and more inti-
mately than are their bodies, and that not by any passing
affection of sense or spirit, but by a deliberate and firm act
of the will; and from this union of souls by God's decree, a
sacred and inviolable bond arises.

Pius XI

LORD, bless this bed
and all who dwell in it,
that there may be found in them
holiness, chastity, meekness,
fulfillment of the law and obedience to God,
Father, Son and Holy Spirit.

Pontifical of Egbert

WHILE the birth of a child is the most dramatic example
of human creative powers, human creative responsibility is a daily task, situated in relationships between persons. Husbands and wives create one another throughout
life. It is their joy and their calling. It has nothing to do with
changing another person but everything to do with allowing a person to develop responsibility as part of a couple.

Robert Crotty and
John Barry Ryan

TWO cups are before you. By your choice, only one is
reserved for the two of you alone. You decided to share
the first cup with those who have been partners in your
lives thus far, the ones who have helped to make you the
individuals you are.

Jewish liturgy

FEW of those who prattle about that "happiest day" seem
to consider the dour expectations this suggests about the
marriage from its second day on. They don't realize that a
wedding reception is basically a large party, and is therefore
not perfectible because there are too many variables, not to
mention too many people who one thought would not
accept. At any rate, someone whose idea of ultimate happiness is a day spent at a big party, even spent being the
center of attention at a marvelous big party, is too young to
get married.

What Miss Manners wishes all brides is not the happiest
days of their lives, but jolly gatherings of family and friends,
in which they are the object of general admiration, but
everyone has a good time. They will then have some happiness left over with which to live happily ever after.

Judith Martin

WHEN I seek divine acceptance,
or implore God's blessing pure,
comes the answer: "Bless each other,
this will heaven's best secure."

Shaker hymn

MAY their life be marked by harmony,
continual charity,
modest chastity,
the attitude of humility,
moral discipline
and the highest beauty of all religiosity.

*The Canterbury*
*Benedictional*

THE pathway of the nuptial life is no longer a simple itin-
erary; it is placed on the road to eternity, and the shared
advance of the couple is therefore like the still point of a
turning wheel.

Paul Evdokimov

DEAREST Lord, teach me to be generous;
Teach me to serve you as you deserve;
To give and not to count the cost,
To fight and not to heed the wounds,
To toil and not to seek for rest,
To labor and not to seek reward,
Save that of knowing that I do your will.

Ignatius Loyola
Sixteenth century

YOU can give one person all your life and not be hungry
or bitter or broke — not ever, right on, far as you go.

Reynolds Price

LOVE is like the wild rose-briar,
Friendship like the holly-tree —
The holly is dark when the rose-briar blooms
But which will bloom most constantly?

The wild rose-briar is sweet in spring,
Its summer blossoms scent the air;
Yet wait till winter comes again
And who will call the wild-briar fair?

Then scorn the silly rose-wreath now
And deck thee with the holly's sheen,
That when December blights thy brow
He still may leave thy garland green.

Emily Brontë
Nineteenth century

HOLY God,
you have crowned your saints
with imperishable crowns
and you have joined heaven and earth.
Bless, then, these crowns
which we are to place on the heads of your servants.
That they may be for them a crown
of glory and honor. Amen.
A crown of salvation and blessing. Amen.
A crown of joy and peace. Amen.
A crown of rejoicing and gladness. Amen.
A crown of virtue and righteousness. Amen.
A crown of wisdom and understanding. Amen.

Coptic liturgy    A crown of strength and firmness. Amen.

EVERYONE then who hears these words of mine and acts on them will be like a wise man who built his house on rock. The rain fell, the floods came, and the winds blew and beat on that house, but it did not fall, because it had been founded on rock. And everyone who hears these words of mine and does not act on them will be like a foolish man who built his house on sand. The rain fell, and the floods came, and the winds blew and beat against that house, and it fell — and great was its fall!

Matthew 7:24 – 27

IT is what happens whenever one person finds in another a new and unknown life: each sees in the other a mysterious life, and each is drawn to the other in the hoping of sharing the other's life. Yet there is death between them, for the new life each sees in the other is like death to the life that is familiar. "They live one another's death and die one another's life." They enter into a friendship, but their friendship is not based on sharing a life that is familiar, like that of two persons who live within the human circle, who live within the same world. Rather, it is based on sharing an unknown life. Each is linked through the other to an unknown world, to a life beyond the familiar, to a life that seems to lie on the other side of death.

John S. Dunne

GRANT, O heavenly Father, that we may so faithfully believe in thee, and so fervently love one another, always living in thy fear, and in the obedience of thy holy law and blessed will, that we, being fruitful in all good works, may lead our life according to thy good pleasure in this transitory world and, after this frail and short life, obtain the true and immortal life, where thou livest and reignest, world without end. Amen.

Thomas Becon
Sixteenth century

Give them grace, when they hurt each other, to recognize and acknowledge their fault, and to seek each other's forgiveness and yours.

*Book of Common Prayer*

As God's chosen ones, holy and beloved, clothe yourselves with compassion, kindness, humility, meekness, and patience. Bear with one another and, if anyone has a complaint against another, forgive each other; just as the Lord has forgiven you, so you also must forgive. Above all, clothe yourselves with love, which binds everything together in perfect harmony. And let the peace of Christ rule in your hearts, to which indeed you were called in the one body.

Colossians 3:12–15

Lord, cleanse the depths within our souls
And bid resentment cease.
Then, bound to all in bonds of love,
Our lives will spread your peace.

Rosamund Herklots

Forgiveness does not mean ignoring what has been done or putting a false label on an evil act. It means, rather, that the evil act no longer remains as a barrier to the relationship. Forgiveness is a catalyst creating the atmosphere necessary for a fresh start and a new beginning. It is the lifting of a burden or the canceling of a debt.

Martin Luther King, Jr.

Forgiveness is the answer to the child's dream of a miracle by which what is broken is made whole again, what is soiled is again made clean. The dream explains why we need to be forgiven, and why we must forgive. In the presence of God, nothing stands between God and us — we are forgiven. But we cannot feel God's presence if anything is allowed to stand between ourselves and others.

Dag Hammarskjöld

NEVERTHELESS, since it is a law of divine Providence in the supernatural order that people do not reap the full fruit of the sacraments which they receive after acquiring the use of reason unless they cooperate with grace, the grace of matrimony will remain for the most part an unused talent hidden in the field unless the parties exercise these supernatural powers and cultivate and develop the seeds of grace they have received.

Pius XI

WATCH yourself, be the first to ask pardon if you both err, and guard against the little piques, misunderstandings, and hasty words that often pave the way for bitter sorrow and regret.

Louisa May Alcott
Nineteenth century

SUCH a silly husband I have
He has forgotten to hold hands.

Gajal song
India

ZIP, zip the valley wind!
Nothing but wind and rain.
In days of peril, in days of dread
It was always 'I and you.'
Now in time of peace, of happiness,
You have cast me aside.

Zip, zip the valley wind
Across the rocky hills.
No grass but is dying,
No tree but is wilting.
You forget my great merits,
Remember only my small faults.

Chou song
Seventh century BCE

I had vowed in front of God and everybody to love and cherish a man of my own choice forever, and I couldn't make good. "I loved this man more than any other person I've ever known," I wept after nine years of marriage. "How could I have stopped? How can I now recoil from his touch? How can he make me feel angry and bitter and bleak instead of full and joyous? Where did it go for God's sake where did it go?" No one had ever suggested to me that "love and cherish" meant "love and cherish on the whole" or "for the most part" or "more often than not" or even "in fits and starts." That much, I found out over the years, I could manage — "the marriage is dead now, of course, but I've lived in it long enough to know that death and resurrection form its characteristic process."

Nancy Mars

EVEN in the most intense activity, this feeling of unreality — in you who have never come "close" to another. The old fairy tale: the one who has been made invisible or transformed into a beast can only regain human shape through somebody else's love.

Dag Hammarskjöld

WE are with one another
sometimes
and there are no smiles
no easy togetherness
only one and one
against the grain
we speak
sometimes and
nothing
is said
but where we are
apart
there is longing
and pain
like arguments within
ourselves
that will not end

Frank Lamond Phillips

Now they were different people as they started back. Four times they had driven along the shore road to-day, each time a different pair. Curiosity, sadness and desire were behind them now; this was a true returning — to themselves and all their past and future and the encroaching presence of tomorrow. He asked her to sit close in the car, and she did, but they did not seem close, because for that you have to seem to be growing closer. Nothing stands still.

F. Scott Fitzgerald

Talking in bed ought to be easiest,
Lying together there goes back so far,
An emblem of two people being honest.

Yet more and more time passes silently.
Outside, the wind's incomplete unrest
Builds and disperses clouds about the sky,

And dark towns heap up on the horizon.
None of this cares for us. Nothing shows why
At this unique distance from isolation

It becomes still more difficult to find
Words at once true and kind,
Or not untrue and not unkind.

Philip Larkin

Our hearts are cold;
Lord, warm them with your selfless love.

Augustine of Hippo
Fourth century

WHEN Jane had finished and come from the kitchen and waited in the door, he was able to see her steadily — a girl not sure she was not alone. He thought, in a rush, "She is not alone; I will stay here, and need her." He could not say it — a blockage, of tenderness, plugged his throat.

She gave him time, demanding (no, allowing) that he name their future effort, tone, rhythm — tonight, years to come.

He was able to say, after swallowing, what she no longer felt the right to say, "Shall we call it a day?"

She shrugged but smiled, gladly feigning fatigue — "Nothing else to call it."

Reynolds Price    Then he stood to join her.

LIKE the bee, we distill poison from honey for our self-defense — what happens to the bee if it uses its sting is

Dag Hammarskjöld    well known.

THE hut is considered the woman's property. This is one of the strongest points a woman has in arguments with her husband. I have seen a woman who has failed to get anywhere in a matrimonial disagreement simply turn around and start methodically pulling the leaves off the hut. Usually the husband stops her halfway. In this case, however, the husband was particularly stubborn. He waited until she had taken all the leaves off, then remarked to the camp at large that his wife was going to be dreadfully cold that night. There was nothing for her to do, without losing face, but to continue; so reluctantly, and very slowly, she started to pull out the sticks that formed the framework of

Colin M. Turnbull    her home.

YOU say you love me, and yet you'll do this to me — rob me of you for ever. I made you with love. I've wept your tears. I've saved you from more than you will ever know; I planted in you this longing for peace only so that one day I could satisfy your longing and watch your happiness. And now you push me away, you put me out of your reach. There are no capital letters to separate us when we talk together. I am not Thou but simply you, when you speak to me; I am humble as any other beggar. Can't you trust me as you'd trust a faithful dog? I have been faithful to you for two thousand years.

So long as you live, the voice said, I have hope.                    Graham Greene

MY dear Eustacia,

I must obey my heart without consulting my reason too closely. Will you come back to me? Do so, and the past shall never be mentioned. I was too severe; but, O, Eustacia, the provocation! You don't know, you never will know, what those words of anger cost me which you drew down upon yourself. All that an honest man can promise you I promise now, which is that from me you shall never suffer anything on this score again. After all the vows we have made, Eustacia, I think we had better pass the remainder of our lives in trying to keep them. Come to me, then, even if you reproach me. I have thought of your sufferings that morning on which I parted from you; I know they were genuine, and they are as much as you ought to bear. Our love must still continue. Such hearts as ours would never have been given us but to be concerned with each other. I could not ask you back at first, Eustacia, for I was unable to persuade myself that he who was with you was not there as a lover. But if you will come and explain distracting appearances I do not question that you can show your honesty to me. Why have you not come before? Do you think I will not listen to you? Surely not, when you remember the kisses and vows we exchanged under the summer moon. Return then, and you shall be warmly welcomed. I can no longer think of you to your prejudice — I am but too much absorbed in justifying you.

— Your husband as ever,                              Thomas Hardy
Clym                                            Nineteenth century

Talmud

THERE is no marriage settlement in which the parties concerned throw no discord.

HE could not feel repentant that he, a handsome amorous man of thirty-four, was not in love with his wife, the mother of five living and two dead children and only a year younger than himself. He repented only of not having managed to conceal his conduct from her. Nevertheless he felt his unhappy position and pitied his wife, his children, and himself. He might perhaps have been able to hide things from her had he known that the knowledge would so distress her. He had never clearly considered the matter, but had a vague notion that his wife had long suspected him of being unfaithful and winked at it. He even thought that she, who was nothing but an excellent mother of a family, worn-out, already growing elderly, no longer pretty, and in no way remarkable — in fact, quite an ordinary woman — ought to be lenient to him, if only from a sense of justice. It turned out that the very opposite was the case.

Leo Tolstoy
Nineteenth century

Eugene Becklard
Nineteenth century

WHEN crossed in love, a woman becomes melancholy, a man insane.

HE knew she'd heard his steps, could hear his near breathing; but she did not look, made no use of her face, relied on the force of her neck and back — the martyr's hunched acceptance. Again he waited for the crush of *something* — revulsion or tenderness. Again nothing fell.

Reynolds Price

WHEN my husband is angry, I keep calm. You see,
when one becomes fire, the other must be water.    Kumut Chandruang

STILL, it is dear defiance now to carry
Fair flags of you above my indignation,
Top, with a pretty glory and a merry
Softness, the scattered pound of my cold passion.
I pull you down my foxhole. Do you mind?
You burn in bits of saucy color then.
I let you flutter out against the pained
Volleys. Against my power crumpled and wan.
You, and the yellow pert exuberance
Of dandelion days, unmocking sun;
The blowing of clear wind in your gay hair;
Love changeful in you (like a music, or
Like a sweet mournfulness, or like a dance,
Or like the tender struggle of a fan).    Gwendolyn Brooks

A good argument, when conducted properly, takes the
time and full attention of two people.    Erma Bombeck

THE incident, of course, gave them the opportunity to
evoke many other trivial quarrels from many other dim
and turbulent dawns. Resentments stirred up other resentments, reopened old scars, turned them into fresh wounds,
and both were dismayed at the desolating proof that in so
many years of conjugal battling they had done little more    Gabriel García
than nurture their rancor.    Márquez

TOGETHER we must plunge
deeper into our pain for more—
for the more pain we attempt to escape
the more joy we automatically negate
for it is through pain that we
ultimately realize the specific beautiful or ugly
innards of
our
Carolyn M. Rodgers    selves.

I grant you, jealousy's a proof of love,
But 'tis a weak and unavailing medicine;
John Dryden    It puts out the disease, and makes it show,
Seventeenth century    But has no power to cure.

IN the cool of the afternoon the fiend from hell specially
sent to lovers arrived at Janie's ear. Doubt. All the fears
that circumstance could provide and the heart feel,
attacked her on every side. This was a new sensation for
her, but no less excruciating. If only Tea Cake would make
her certain! He did not return that night nor the next and so
she plunged into the abyss and descended to the ninth
Zora Neale Hurston    darkness where light has never been.

WE cannot afford to forget any experience, not even
Dag Hammarskjöld    the most painful.

WHEN they recalled this episode, now they had rounded the corner of old age, neither could believe the astonishing truth that this had been the most serious argument in fifty years of living together, and the only one that had made them both want to abandon their responsibilities and begin a new life. Even when they were old and placid they were careful about bringing it up, for the barely healed wounds could begin to bleed again as if they had been inflicted only yesterday.

Gabriel García
Márquez

YOU glow in my heart
Like the flames of uncounted candles.
But when I go to warm my hands,
My clumsiness overturns the light,
And then I stumble
Against the tables and chairs.

Amy Lowell

BELOVED, let us love one another, because love is from God; everyone who loves is born of God and knows God. Whoever does not love does not know God, for God is love. God's love was revealed among us in this way: God sent his only Son into the world so that we might live through him. In this is love, not that we loved God but that he loved us and sent his Son to be the atoning sacrifice for our sins. Beloved, since God loved us so much, we also ought to love one another.

1 John 4:7 – 11

*Book of Common Prayer*

MAKE their life together a sign of Christ's love to this sinful and broken world, that unity may overcome estrangement, forgiveness heal guilt, and joy conquer despair.

*Matthew 5:13 – 16*

YOU are the salt of the earth; but if salt has lost its taste, how can its saltiness be restored? It is no longer good for anything, but is thrown out and trampled under foot.

You are the light of the world. A city built on a hill cannot be hid. No one after lighting a lamp puts it under the bushel basket, but on the lampstand, and it gives light to all in the house. In the same way, let your light shine before others, so that they may see your good works and give glory to your Father in heaven.

*Roman liturgy*

HOLY Father, you created humankind in your
own image
and made man and woman to be joined as husband
and wife
in union of body and heart
and so fulfill their mission in this world.

*Erskine Peters*

MARRIAGE is unity for making, say the knowledge-holders. In making is the power of energy.

IT is important to realize from the outset that marriage was originally considered a "Christian marriage," or a marriage contracted and lived "in the Lord," because it was a marriage between two baptized believers in Christ. In other words, the sacramentality of marriage as a *state* depended not on a wedding rite but on the baptismal identity of the couple. Their life together was a form of the Christian life, a form which, in the mutual love and reciprocal service for which marriage afforded occasion, was capable of iconicizing the mutual relationship between Christ and the church.

Mark Searle

THIS, then, is what it means to marry in Christ: spiritual marriage is like spiritual birth, which is not of blood, nor of the will of the flesh.

John Chrysostum
Fourth century

LET us love, not in word or speech, but in truth and action. And by this we will know that we are from the truth and will reassure our hearts before him whenever our hearts condemn us; for God is greater than our hearts, and he knows everything. Beloved, if our hearts do not condemn us, we have boldness before God; and we receive from him whatever we ask, because we obey his commandments and do what pleases him.

1 John 3:18–22

IT is only by rising above the philosophy of the "common good" that one can grasp the singular worth of those who love each other. It is this hidden and intimate element that is consecrated in the sacrament, it is love that constitutes its matter and receives the gift of the Holy Spirit, the nuptial Pentecost. Society knows but the surface. Between the two lovers there is only God who is the third term; this is why the meaning of marriage is taken precisely in this dual and direct relation to God.

Olivier Clement

THE rite of marriage, like all liturgical rites, expresses the paschal mystery of Christ: his life, death and resurrection. This is the primary meaning of the sacrament of marriage, and this must be evident in its celebration.

The core of the paschal mystery is the acceptance of God's love by the humanity of Christ. The love of God can be experienced in many ways. The most notable of these ways in human affairs is the love of a man and a woman. It is most notable, for it involves one's whole being, body, mind and spirit, in a relationship that is found wherever human beings are found.

Marriage, then, by its position in the order of creation, is already a sacrament: it is the most powerful symbol of God's love for the world. God's love is all-embracing: it sets us free to love the world in our turn. Married love, as its symbol, reflects the expansiveness of God's love. It cannot become so intimate and exclusive that it ceases to be love at all. The celebration of marriage in the Christian Church must not be allowed to reflect anything but the fullest meaning of human love.

*Roman liturgy*
*Canada*

CAMELS and mules behave more decently than some people at wedding receptions! Is marriage a comedy? It is a mystery, an image of something far greater. If you have no respect for marriage, at least respect what it symbolizes: "This is a great mystery, and I take it to mean Christ and the church."

*John Chrysostom*
*Fourth century*

ON the third day there was a wedding in Cana of Galilee, and the mother of Jesus was there. Jesus and his disciples had also been invited to the wedding. When the wine gave out, the mother of Jesus said to him, "They have no wine." And Jesus said to her, "Woman, what concern is that to you and to me? My hour has not yet come." His mother said to the servants, "Do whatever he tells you." Now standing there were six stone water jars for the Jewish rites of purification, each holding twenty or thirty gallons. Jesus said to them, "Fill the jars with water." And they filled them up to the brim. He said to them, "Now draw some out, and take it to the chief steward." So they took it. When the steward tasted the water that had become wine, and did not know where it came from (though the servants who had drawn the water knew), the steward called the bridegroom and said to him, "Everyone serves the good wine first, and then the inferior wine after the guests have become drunk. But you have kept the good wine until now." Jesus did this, the first of his signs, in Cana of Galilee, and revealed his glory; and his disciples believed in him.

John 2:1 – 11

COUPLES are reminded that their marriage is an act of public worship, and as such should be celebrated in the place where the local community usually gathers to celebrate.

Roman liturgy
Canada

MARRIAGE continues long after the celebration is over, and those couples who keep coming to the eucharist to give thanks for "growing old together" witness to an ancient tradition whereby marriage anniversaries are brought into the ambit of a special gathering at the Lord's Table.

Kenneth W. Stevenson

WHERE true love and charity are found,
      God is there.
Therefore, when we gather as one.
Let us be as one in the Lord.
May careless thought, action, or deed not divide us;
Let Christ, our God, dwell among us, in our hearts.

Latin office hymn

MAKE my joy complete: be of the same mind, having the same love, being in full accord and of one mind. Do nothing from selfish ambition or conceit, but in humility regard others as better than yourselves. Let each of you look not to your own interests, but to the interests of others. Let the same mind be in you that was in Christ Jesus,

who, though he was in the form of.God,
    did not regard equality with God
    as something to be exploited,
but emptied himself,
    taking the form of a slave,
    being born in human likeness.
And being found in human form,
    he humbled himself
    and became obedient to the point of death —
    even death on a cross.
Therefore God also highly exalted him
    and gave him the name
    that is above every name,
so that at the name of Jesus
    every knee should bend,
    in heaven and on earth and under the earth,
and every tongue should confess
    that Jesus Christ is Lord,
Philippians 2:2 – 11    to the glory of God the Father.

REAL love, as it is lived out by Christ and his followers, leads to life, more and more abundant life. And love
Roman liturgy
Canada    never fails, never falters: it is stronger than death.

COME slowly — Eden!
Lips unused to Thee —
Bashful — sip thy Jessamines —
As the fainting Bee —

Reaching late his flower,
Round her chamber hums —
Counts his nectars —
Enters — and is lost in Balms.

*Emily Dickinson*
*Nineteenth century*

THE mutuality of their delight in one another, the totality
of their self-giving, and the finality of the love itself,
which seems in no way oriented toward the producing of
children or the continuation of the tribe, are a celebration
of equality between the man and the woman.

*Sandra M. Schneiders*

A human intimacy — free from the earth, but blessing
the earth.

*Dag Hammarskjöld*

O God of love, inspire our life,
reveal your will in all we do;
join every husband, every wife
in mutual love and love for you.

*Russell Schulz-Widmar*

CALL the needy children home,
make a feast that they may share;
Not the worldly wise and whole
need the Good Physician's care.
'Tis the mission of God's love
to reclaim, restore, redeem,
Give full interest, joy and love,
life and labor to this theme.

*Shaker hymn*

RABBI Aha said: If a man marries a godly wife, it is as though he had fulfilled the whole Torah from beginning to end. To him applies, "Thy wife is like a fruitful vine." Therefore the verses of the chapter of the virtuous wife in Proverbs are arranged in complete alphabetical sequence (and no letter is missing, as in other alphabets in the Bible) from *Alef* to *Tau*. It is solely for the merit of the righteous women in each generation that each generation is redeemed.

*Talmud*

THE days are surely coming, says the LORD when I will make a new covenant with the house of Israel and the house of Judah. It will not be like the covenant that I made with their ancestors when I took them by the hand to bring them out of the land of Egypt — a covenant that they broke, though I was their husband, says the LORD. But this is the covenant that I will make with the house of Israel after those days, says the LORD: I will put my law within them, and I will write it on their hearts; and I will be their God, and they shall be my people.

*Jeremiah 31:31 – 33*

THE house of our father Abraham was blessed by the three men who visited him; the house of Zeccai was blessed by the presence of Christ who is the Bridegroom of Truth; and now we pray you, O Lord, that the Holy Trinity may dwell in your servants' house that it may be blessed in the generations of the just.

*Syrian Orthodox liturgy*

WE bless you, Lord, God of Israel,
who have shown mercy to your two servants.
Make them bless you more and more,
and offer you a sacrifice of praise,
that all the nations may know
that you alone are Lord,

*Visigothic Liber*
*Antiphonarius*
glorious over all the earth.

WE also pledge to establish a home open to the spiritual potential in all life; a home wherein the flow of the seasons and the passages of life are celebrated through the symbols of our Jewish heritage; a home filled with reverence for learning, loving and generosity; a home wherein ancient melody, candles and wine sanctify the table; a home joined ever more closely to the community of Israel.

Gustav Buchdahl,
Lawrence Kushner and
Bernard H. Mehlman

THE earthly love between you has been overlaid by the supernatural love of Christ for the church. Your new fellowship is a spectacle pleasing to God and to angels, for it is a union which surpasses all others, destined as it is to populate the church of God in heaven and on earth.

Roman liturgy

IN its full measure, grace comes at the end of a sacrifice. The spouses themselves receive it from the moment they undertake to present themselves before the Father in heaven in their dignity as priests, and to offer to God the sacrifice in Christ, the "reasonable gift," the oblation of their entire nuptial life.

Paul Evdokimov

MARRIAGE, like monasticism, is a sign of God's reign, because it begins to restore the unity of humankind (and the cosmos as a whole) which has been broken up by sin. Thus marriage is both a great mystery in itself and represents a greater mystery, the unity of redeemed humankind in Christ.

Catharine P. Roth

MARRIAGE is a sacrament similar to the eucharist, which is a sacrament not only when it is being effected, but also so long as it endures. For so long as the married parties are alive, so long is their union a sacrament of Christ and the church.

Robert Bellarmine
Sixteenth century

Syrian Orthodox liturgy

Oᴜʀ Lord Jesus Christ, who was crowned with a crown of thorns, and destroyed the powers of Satan, bless your servants as you blessed our father Adam and our mother Eve, and Seth, Noah, Abraham, and Sarah, Isaac and Rebecca, Jacob and Rachel, Joseph and Asiath, and David who was king, prophet and singer of your holy church. Make them, O Lord, a blessed couple, emulous of good works of righteousness. By laying aside these temporary crowns, make them worthy, O Lord, to be among the guests at your heavenly table who are worthy of that everlasting and imperishable crown.

UɴɪQᴜᴇ to the Coptic rite is the anointing of the bride and groom. The anointing precedes the crowning, which is the key element of the Coptic liturgy as it is of all Eastern marriage rites. The symbolism is distinctly different from that of the Byzantine crowning, however, for the crowns here represent the blessings of God in this world and in the world to come. The meaning of the whole liturgy is summed up in the coronation chant: "The Father blesses, the Son crowns, the Spirit sanctifies and makes perfect." Through the ritual, the bride and groom themselves become symbols, not only assuming their place in salvation history after the great couples of the past, but actually assuming the role of the lovers in the Song of Songs, of the divine Word and the Virgin Mother, of Christ and the church.

Mark Searle and
Kenneth W. Stevenson

Iᴛ is you, my spouse, whom I desire. In searching for you I struggle and I am crucified with you. I am buried with you in baptism, and I suffer with you only to live with you.

Troparion of the
Holy Martyrs

THE setting of ancient wedding rings showed two profiles joined by a cross. Perfect love is love crucified. This is why the crowns refer to the Lord's crown of thorns, the only one that can give meaning to all others. Throughout their entire life, the spouses will hear echoes, strong or dim, of the Troparion of the Holy Martyrs.

Paul Evdokimov

AFTER the cloud embankments,
The lamentation of wind,
And the starry descent into time,
We came to the flashing waters and shaded our eyes
From the glare.

Alone with the shore and the harbor,
The stems of the coconut trees,
The fronds of silence and hushed music,
We cried for the new revelation
And waited for miracles to rise.

Where elements touch and merge,
Where shadows swoon like outcasts on the sand
And the tired moment waits, its courage gone —
There were we

In latitudes where storms are born.

Arna Bontemps

TO believe a being partakes of an unknown life into which love would lead us, this is, of all that must be before love will come to birth, the one thing most needed, and it makes the rest easy.

Marcel Proust

FOR this is one of the miracles of love; it gives — to both, but perhaps especially to the woman — a power of seeing through its own enchantments and yet not being disenchanted.

C. S. Lewis

IN the catacombs, the most frequent image is the figure of a woman in prayer, the *Orant;* she represents the one true attitude of the human soul. It is not enough to *say* prayers; one must become, *be* prayer, prayer incarnate. It is not enough to have moments of praise. All of life, each act, every gesture, even the smile of the human face, must become a hymn of adoration, an offering, a prayer. One should offer not what one has, but what one is.

Paul Evdokimov

THERE were pure kinds of work that involved no products so were hardest of all, being fueled by nothing more visible than love. These scenes will be a chart of one kind, a work of love which will find exactly that — that love can be work.

Reynolds Price

LORD, behold our family here assembled.
We thank you for this place in which we dwell,
for the love that unites us,
for the peace accorded us this day,
for the hope with which we expect the morrow;
for the health, the work, the food and the bright skies
that make our lives delightful;
for our friends in all parts of the earth.
Give us courage and gaiety and the quiet mind.
Spare us to our friends, soften us to our enemies.
Bless us, if it may be, in all our innocent endeavors;
if it may not, give us the strength
to endure that which is to come
that we may be brave in peril,
constant in tribulation, temperate in wrath
and in all changes of fortune
and down to the gates of death,
loyal and loving to one another.
We beseech of you this help and mercy
for Christ's sake.

Robert Louis Stevenson
Nineteenth century

BESTOW on them, if it is your will, the gift and heritage of children and the grace to bring them up to know you, to love you, and to serve you.

*Book of Common Prayer*

BLESS them who are joined
in accordance with your will.
May they multiply like our first fathers,
Abraham, Isaac, and Jacob, whom you blessed.
Bless them like Abraham and Sarah.
Exalt them like Isaac and Rebecca.
May they multiply as you multiplied Jacob and his seed.
Glorify them as you glorified Joseph in Egypt,
and make them chaste as he.
Make them numerous, as you did Elkana and Anna,
whom you blessed with the joy of a child,
the faithful Samuel, the prophet.
Make them worthy
of the visitation of your holy archangel,
as happened to Zachary and Elizabeth,
to whom you gave the grace of bearing him
who is the greatest born of woman,
John the Baptist,
forerunner of your only Son.
You also blessed Joachim and Anna,
Lord our Master,
for from them was born the spiritual ark,
Mary, Mother of God.
In her your only Son became flesh.

*Coptic liturgy*

THE child born of this nuptial community prolongs it and reaffirms the already perfectly realized unity. Love contemplates its reflection in the world and begets the child.

*Paul Evdokimov*

THESE are the two purposes for which marriage was instituted: to make us chaste, and to make us parents. Of these two, the reason of chastity takes precedence. When desire began, then marriage also began. It sets a limit to desire by teaching us to keep to one wife. Marriage does not always lead to child-bearing, although there is the word of God which says, "Be fruitful and multiply, and fill the earth." We have as witnesses all those who are married but childless. So the purpose of chastity takes precedence, especially now, when the whole world is filled with our kind.

John Chrysostom
Fourth century

MARRIAGE: that I call the will of two to create the one who is more than those who created it. Reverence before one another, as before the willers of such a will — that I call marriage.

Friedrich Nietzsche
Nineteenth century

HOW good to revere the Lord,
to walk in God's path.

Your table rich from labor —
how good for you!
Your beloved, a fruitful vine
in the warmth of your home.

Like olive shoots,
children surround your table.
This is your blessing
when you revere the Lord.

May the Lord bless you from Zion!
May you see Jerusalem prosper
every day of your life.
May you see your children's children,
and on Israel, peace!

Psalm 128

T HE crowning also signifies the royal dignity of the family life: the spouses are crowned in glory as potential parents; they are now responsible in ruling their household according to the will of God.

Athenagoras
Kokkinakis

C HRIST was invited to the wedding feast with his disciples, not merely to take part in the rejoicing, but in order to work a miracle, and to sanctify the act of human generation in its very source.

Cyril of Alexandria
Fifth century

U P the stairs I ran to the wan mother and whimpering babe, to the sanctuary on whose altar a life at my bidding had offered itself to win a life, and won. What is this tiny, formless thing, this newborn wail from an unknown world — all head and voice? I handle it curiously, and watch perplexed its winking, breathing, and sneezing. I did not love it then; it seemed a ludicrous thing to love; but her I loved, my girl-mother, she whom I now saw unfolding like the glory of the morning — the transfigured woman. Through her I came to love the wee thing, as it grew strong; as its little soul unfolded itself in twitter and cry and half-formed word, and as its eyes caught the gleam and flash of life.

W. E. B. DuBois

L ET the sweetness of your blessing
so surround them
that whatever children may be born of their union
may find favor with their fellows
and be blessed by you.

Liber Ordinum

Because of their importance, we must not neglect our homes in the rapid changes of the present day. For when tests of character come in later years, strength to the good will not come from the modern improvements or amusements few may have enjoyed but from the quiet moments and the "still small voices" of the old home.

Nothing ever can take the place of this early home influence; and as it does not depend upon externals, it may be the possession of the poor as well as of the rich, a heritage from all fathers and mothers to their children.

*Laura Ingalls Wilder*

Through their devout love and unwearying care, the home, though it suffer the want and hardship of this valley of tears, may become for the children in its own way a foretaste of that paradise of delight in which the Creator placed the first members of the human race.

*Pius XI*

The Israelites say to God, "Yea, we recognize you as Father. Like an orphan girl, who was brought up by a good and faithful guardian, who looked after her well. He sought to give her in marriage, and the scribe came to write the marriage contract. He said to her, 'What is your name?' She told him. 'What is your father's name?' She was silent. 'Why are you silent?' said her guardian. She said, 'Because I know none other than you as my father, for he who brings up is father, not he who begets.'"

*Talmud*

Christian couples are, for each other, for their children, and for their relatives, cooperators of grace and witnesses of the faith. They are the first to pass on the faith to their children and to dedicate them in it. By word and example, they form them to a Christian and apostolic life; they offer them wise guidance in the choice of vocation, and if they discover in them a sacred vocation they encourage it with all care.

*Constitution on the Church in the Modern World*

A CROSS the years, the old home and its love called to me, and memories of sweet words of counsel came flooding back. I realize that all my life the teachings of those early days have influenced me, and the example set by Father and Mother has been something I have tried to follow, with failures here and there, with rebellion at times; but always coming back to it as the compass needle to the star.

Laura Ingalls Wilder

Y OU have joined people in marriage
    with the sweet yoke of concord
and the unbreakable bond of peace,
so that the chaste fruitfulness of holy marriages
may serve to increase the adoptive children of God.
Your providence, O Lord, and your grace
serve to guide both things in wonderful ways:
what generation brings forth to enrich the world,
regeneration leads to the increase of the church.

*Gregorian
Sacramentary*

M AY your life together
    be like the fragrance of the lilies,
that your minds might rise easily
to heaven at all times.
May you remain true,
with God's help,
to the exchange of pledges you have made
that they might be signs of united hearts
and that you might be the parents of virtuous children.

*Liber Ordinum*

LET us join together
and beget our little ones.
Loving each other,
With genial minds and hearts,
May we live
Hindu liturgy    Through a hundred autumns.

MAY they be loved by all,
May they beget fathers and mothers,
Masai Tribe    May they have goats and cattle,
Kenya and Tanzania    May they beget children.

AFTER Sam was born, I remember thinking that no one
had ever told me how much I would love my child;
now, of course, I realized something else no one tells you:
that a child is a grenade. When you have a baby, you set off
an explosion in your marriage, and when the dust settles,
your marriage is different from what it was. Not better, nec-
Nora Ephron    essarily; not worse, necessarily; but different.

Navajo saying    A man can't get rich if he takes proper care of his family.

Talmud    YOUR own offspring teaches you reason.

So sturdy and masterful he grew, so filled with bubbling life, so tremulous with the unspoken wisdom of a life but eighteen months distant from the All-life — we were not far from worshiping this revelation of the divine, my wife and I.

W. E. B. DuBois

I loved all my children, but this girl child was precious in a special way that had brought me closer to all three. Life and death. Pain and joy. Having and losing. You couldn't experience one without the other. Background and foreground. The presence of my daughter would always remind me that things didn't have to be the way they were. We could have lost her. Could lose her today. And that was the way it would always be. Ebb and flow. Touch and go. Her arrival shattered complacency. When I looked in her eyes I was reminded to love her and treasure her and all the people I loved because nothing could be taken for granted.

John Edgar Wideman

*Book of Common Prayer*

GIVE them such fulfillment of their mutual affection that they may reach out in love and concern for others.

LET love be genuine; hate what is evil, hold fast to what is good; love one another with mutual affection; outdo one another in showing honor. Do not lag in zeal, be ardent in spirit, serve the Lord. Rejoice in hope, be patient in suffering, persevere in prayer. Contribute to the needs of the saints; extend hospitality to strangers.

Bless those who persecute you; bless and do not curse them. Rejoice with those who rejoice, weep with those who weep. Live in harmony with one another; do not be haughty, but associate with the lowly; do not claim to be wiser than you are. Do not repay anyone evil for evil, but take thought for what is noble in the sight of all. If it is possible, so far as it depends on you, live peaceably with all.

*Romans 12:9 – 18*

DO not worry, saying, "What will we eat?" or "What will we drink?" or "What will we wear?" For it is the Gentiles who strive for all these things; and indeed your heavenly Fathers knows that you need all these things. But strive first for the kingdom of God and his righteousness, and all those things will be given to you as well.

*Matthew 6:31 – 33*

*Kenneth W. Stevenson*

MARRIAGE is also about the rest of the church.

A couple that love one another, practice mutual forgiveness, care for their elderly and their young, and are sensitive to the needs of others continue the work of Jesus and thereby truly make marriage a sacrament of God's love.

*Robert Crotty and John Barry Ryan*

TRUE love is fruitful. But this fruitfulness is not only expressed through the child; it can also be manifested through hospitality, through service and sometimes through a common creation.

Olivier Clement

THE renewal of Christian marriage, then, would seem to be inseparable, finally, from the renewal of baptismal consciousness and from the profound consequences that will flow therefrom not only for the life of the family, but for the structures of the church itself. Thus we shall have come full circle, back to the baptismal foundations of "marriage in Christ" with which the church's theology of marriage began.

Mark Searle

THE eyes of all look to you,
you give them food in due time.
You open wide your hand
to feed all living things.

Psalm 145:15 – 16

NOTHING if not utterly in death
So let us now demur flowers
Say you saw us in patience
Gently remove wrath from thorn
And nod "Morning" to moon passing

Happy if merely knowing light
I cannot grasp substances, but
If by chance, I drop my world
And hear it smash in the basin
I rejoice in the sound, if not fancy.

Let it stand at that. If with
These eyes I encourage the
Great Distances to move closer
and sit here with me in silence
Then will such bright candles as these
Be not held hostages too soon.

James P. Vaughn

THE groom and bride have also promised each other to strive throughout their lives together to achieve an openness which will enable them to share their thoughts, their feelings, and their experiences.

To be sensitive at all times to each others' needs, to attain mutual intellectual, emotional, physical, and spiritual fulfillment. To work for the perpetuation of Judaism and of the Jewish people in their home, in their family life, and in their communal endeavors.

Bernhard H. Mehlman,
Gustav Buchdahl and
Eugene R. Lipman

LET Israel trust God,
their help and shield.
Let the house of Aaron trust God,
their help and shield.
Let all believers trust God,
their help and shield.

Psalm 115:9 – 11

GO work in my vineyard today, saith the Lord,
The hungry and thirsty are there;
go scatter the seed of true faith far abroad
And call in the needy to share.
Cast out in my name all the errors of earth,
Go toil where afflictions abound,
Go publish the light which perfects the new birth,
The light a full Savior is found.

Shaker hymn

Dear Lord! kind Lord!
Gracious Lord! I pray
Thou wilt look on all I love
Tenderly to-day!
Weed their hearts of weariness;
Scatter every care
Down a wake of angel-wings
Winnowing the air.

Bring unto the sorrowing
All release from pain;
Let the lips of laughter
Overflow again;
And with all the needy
O divide, I pray,
This vast treasure of content
That is mine to-day!

James Whitcomb Riley
Nineteenth century

Of all the women
Of all the world
Delicate
In their various encasings
Of body
Of mind
This one
Bent asleep before me
On the bed
Is the one through whom all must be loved
As I have promised

Norman Fischer

HALLELUJAH!
Happy those who love God
and delight in the law.
Their children shall be blest,
strong and upright in the land.

Their households thrive,
their integrity stands firm.
A light shines on them in darkness,
a God of mercy and justice.

The good lend freely
and deal fairly,
they will never stumble;
their justice shall be remembered.

Bad news holds no power,
strong hearts trust God.
Steady and fearless,
they look down on their enemy.

They support the poor,
their integrity stands firm,
their strength brings them honor.

Psalm 112:1 – 9

MAY the peace of Christ live always in your hearts and
in your home.
May you have true friends to stand by you, both in joy
and in sorrow.
May you be ready and willing to help and comfort all who
come to you in need.
And may the blessings promised to the compassionate be
yours in abundance.

Roman liturgy

GIVE us, Lord, a bit o' sun,
a bit o' work and a bit o' fun;
give us all in the struggle and sputter
our daily bread and a bit o' butter;
give us health, our keep to make,
an' a bit to spare for others' sake;
give us sense, for we're some of us duffers,
an' a heart to feel for all that suffers;
give us, too, a bit of a song
and a tale, and a book to help us along.
An' give us our share o' sorrow's lesson
that we may prove how grief's a blessin'.
Give us, Lord, a chance to be
our goodly best, brave, wise, and free,
our goodly best for ourself, and others,
till all men learn to live as brothers.

From the wall
of an old inn
Lancaster, England

IF you are inclined to entertain and give dinner parties,
there should be nothing immodest or excessive about
them. And if you should find some poor, saintly man who
just by stepping into your house would bring God's blessing
upon you, invite him.

John Chrysostom
Fourth century

FILL my house unto the fullest.
Eat my bread and drink my wine
The love I bear is held from no one.
All I have and all I do
I give to you.

Peter Kearney

O living bread, that came down from heaven to give life to the world! O loving shepherd of our souls, from your throne of glory whence, a "hidden God," you pour out your grace on families and peoples, we commend to you particularly the sick, the unhappy, the poor and all who beg for food and employment, imploring for all and every one the assistance of your providence; we commend to you the families, so that they may be fruitful centers of Christian life. May the abundance of your grace be poured out over all.

John XXIII

THE love of husband and wife is the force that welds society together.

John Chrysostom
Fourth century

LORD, in their change, let frost and heat,
And winds and dews be giv'n;
All fostering power, all influence sweet,
Breathe from the bounteous heav'n.
Attemper fair with gentle air
The sunshine and the rain,
That kindly earthy with timely birth
May yield her fruits again:

That we may feed the poor aright,
And, gath'ring round thy throne,
Here, in the holy angels' sight,
Repay thee of thine own:
That we may praise thee all our days,
And with the Father's Name,
And with the Holy Spirit's gifts,
The Saviour's love proclaim.

Edward White Benson
Nineteenth century

FILL their houses with wheat, grain and oil
and with every good thing,
so that they may give in turn to those in need.          Byzantine liturgy

GRATITUDE and readiness. You got all for nothing. Do not
hesitate, when it is asked for, to give your all, which,
in fact, is nothing, for all.          Dag Hammarskjöld

IF God loves the ones we can't," she said, "then finally
maybe we can."          Wendell Berry

BUILD houses and live in them; plant gardens and eat what
they produce. Take wives and have sons and daughters;
take wives for your sons, and give your daughters in marriage, that they may bear sons and daughters; multiply
there, and do not decrease. But seek the welfare of the city
where I have sent you into exile, and pray to the LORD on its
behalf, for in its welfare you will find your welfare.          Jeremiah 29:5 – 7

Roman liturgy

MAY they reach old age in the company of their friends, and come at last to the kingdom of heaven.

GROW old along with me!
The best is yet to be,
The last of life, for which the first was made:
Our times are in His hand

Robert Browning
Nineteenth century

Who saith "A whole I planned,
Youth shows but half; trust God: see all, nor be afraid!"

GRANT them to enjoy length of days in this life and to desire the unending life that is to come. Let them so negotiate all temporal business that they will continue faithfully to long for eternal things. May they handle the goods that pass away in such manner as not to lose those that abide. Serving you in fidelity and truth, let them see their children's children that, after a long life in this present

Visigothic liturgy

world, they may attain to the kingdom of heaven.

FOR every generation weddings are a glimpse into the future, a repudiation of past griefs, and a celebration of

Anita Diamant

the here and now.

LOOK down, O Lord,
from your holy heaven upon this marriage.
Just as you sent your holy angel Raphael,
to Tobias and Sarah, the daughter of Raguel,
so Lord deign to send your blessing
upon these young people,
that they might remain in your will,
persevere in your will,
live in your love,
increase and grow old,

Benedictional of
Robert of Jumieges

and be multiplied unto length of days.

ON the day of your wedding, so long past, grace was laid up in your souls through the sacrament which you administered to each other. Today you stand before the world as a striking testimony of what God's grace, conferred in matrimony, can effect in the husband and wife who will work along with the divine treasure that is in them. Our world has great need of the living sermon which your example of fidelity and loyalty dins into its ears.     Roman liturgy

TODAY is the forty-eighth anniversary of our Wedding Day — June 22, 1915. I caught the westbound Texas Pacific train that afternoon for Alexandria. I wore a two-piece dress of white Indian Head, a Norfolk jacket and gored white skirt trimmed in green — I made it! My hat was of white fabric — a little roll-brim affair. All quite casual. I don't remember the shoes (probably white) or purse.

Mama drove me to the train. As it passed the gin where papa was working, I waved to him. He held up the hammer he was using in a sort of salute.

A very short ride to Alexandria! I was met by Dave and his friend from Pineville. Dave looked terrible; he had been sick and was still yellow from jaundice. We drove immediately to the parsonage of the minister, Rev. Smith, of the Christian church. Mrs. Smith and Ora Mae Galloway from Bunkie were witnesses to the brief ceremony in the parsonage parlor. I recall that Rev. Smith wished us well and remarked that no couple he ever married had separated or divorced. We took a taxi from there straight to Jena.     Berta Mae Hall Woods

WHEN you came, you were like red wine and honey,
    And the taste of you burnt my mouth with
  its sweetness.
Now you are like morning bread,
Smooth and pleasant.
I hardly taste you at all for I know your savor,
But I am completely nourished.

Amy Lowell

IF ever two were one, then surely we.
If ever man were lov'd by wife, then thee;
If ever wife was happy in a man,
Compare with me ye women if you can.
I prize thy love more than whole mines of gold,
Or all the riches that the East doth hold.
My love is such that rivers cannot quench,

Nor aught but love from thee, give recompense.
Thy love is such I can no way repay,
The heavens reward thee manifold, I pray.
Then while we live, in love lets so persever
That, when we live no more, we may live ever.

Anne Bradstreet
Seventeenth century

THINK we have had a clear and glorious day
And Heaven did kindly to delay the storm,
Just till our close of evening. Ten years' love,
And not a moment lost, but all improved
To the utmost joys — what ages have we lived?

John Dryden
Seventeenth century

BUT in the crowding darkness not a word did they say.
Though the pretty-coated birds had piped so lightly
all the day.
And he had seen the lovers in the little side streets.
And she had heard the morning stories clogged with
sweets.

It was quite a time for loving. It was midnight. It was May.
But in the crowding darkness not a word did they say.

Gwendolyn Brooks

I have seen a line of snow-white birds
Drawn across an evening sky.
I have seen divine, unspoken words
Shining in a lover's eye.
I have seen moonlight on a mountaintop,
Silver and cool and still.
I have heard church bell faintly echoing
Over a distant hill.
Close enough to beauty I have been,
And, in all the whole wide land,
Here's the sweetest sight that I have seen —
One old couple walking hand in hand.

Oscar Hammerstein II

WISH for nothing lest you mar
The perfection in these eyes
Whose entire devotion lies
At the mercy of your will;
Tempt not your sworn comrade, — only
    As I am can I
    Love you as you are —
For my company be lonely
    For my health be ill:
I will sing if you will cry
        . . . I

Never hope to say farewell,
For our lethargy is such
Heaven's kindness cannot touch
Nor earth's frankly brutal drum;
This was long ago decided,
    Both of us know why,
    Can, alas, foretell,
When our falsehoods are divided,
    What we shall become,
One evaporating sigh
        . . . I

W. H. Auden

HERE from the start, from our first of days, look:
I have carved out our lives in secret on this stock
of mountain mahogany the length of your arms
outstretched, the wood clear red, so hard and rare.
It is time to touch and handle what we know we share.

Near the butt, this intricate notch where the grains
converge and join: it is our wedding.
I can read it through with a thumb and tell you now
who danced, who made up the songs, who meant us joy.
These little arrowheads along the grain,
they are the births of our children. See,
they make a kind of design with these heavy crosses,
the deaths of our parents, the loss of friends.

Over it all as it goes, of course, I
have chiseled Events, History — random
hashmarks cut against the swirling grain.
See, here is the Year the World Went Wrong,
we thought, and here the days the Great Men fell.
The lengthening runes of our lives run through it all.

See, our tally stick is whittled nearly end to end;
delicate as scrimshaw, it would not bear you up.
Regrets have polished it, hand over hand.
Yet let us take it up, and as our fingers
like children leading on a trail cry back
our unforgotten wonders, sign after sign,
we will talk softly as of ordinary matters,
and in one another's blameless eyes go blind.

Jarold Ramsey

I am glad, Dear One, that I have known
So much of vagrant love;
Each ephemeral travesty
Has but served to prove
That this which has grown
Oakwise with time,
Storm tested by you and me
Is, and ever shall be
The gift sublime,
The intransmutable verity.

Bessie Calhoun Bird

H E was aware that he did not love her. He had married
her because he liked her haughtiness, her seriousness,
her strength, and also because of some vanity on his part,
but as she kissed him for the first time he was sure there
would be no obstacle to their inventing true love. They did
not speak of it that first night, when they spoke of everything until dawn, nor would they ever speak of it. But in the
long run, neither of them had made a mistake.

Gabriel García
Márquez

N OW, children, years and many rooms away,
and tired with experience, we climb the stairs
to our well-furnished room; undress, and say
familiar words for love; and from the cares

that back us, turn together and once more seek
the warmth of wonder each to the other meant
so strong ago, and with known bodies speak
the unutterable language of content.

Maurice Lindsay

THE moon throws back sunlight into the woods,
but whiter, cleansed by its bounce
amid the cold stars, and the owls
fly their unthinkable paths to pluck
the bleached shrew from her bed of leaves.
Dreaming rotates us, but fear
leads us to cling each to each as a spar
is clung to by the shipwrecked
till dawn brings sky-fire and rescue.

Your breathing, relaxed to its center,
scrapes like a stone on rough fiber,
over and over. Your skin, steeped
in its forgetting, sweats,
and flurries of footwork bring you near
the surface; but then your rapt lungs slip
with a sigh back into the healing,
that unpoliced swirling of spirit
John Updike    whose sharing is a synonym for love.

LIKE us, the squashes in the garden, battered
by rain, have grown bulbous, warty,
speckled and rayed, mushy where they sat too long.
Surrounded by men in tall red hats, the pope
declares married couples can commit adultery
even with each other if lust is in their hearts.
Come here, I say. O, Love, the teenage me
spent days devouring *The Ideal Marriage,*
*Its Physiology and Technique* with matrimony
never once in mind. What diagrams, fabulous plumbing,
faucets, union joints! Then the wild surmise, the ocean
of the little death! I shouldn't forget my fear either,
but mostly I remember the desire rolled tight in a ball.
And the sunny smell of your sheets, the Siamese kittens

playing under the bed, the hummingbirds hovering
at the ruby feeder. Since then the seasons have
   rained down,
children born, lost. So now I can no longer tell you
from the gesture you make with your hand. Our veins
have risen to the surface; our skin become smoke.
The garden lies dusted with snow, a not-so-little death.
Come, let us find a vegetable love, a pumpkin lust
which can last through years and years.                  Hunt Hawkins

N OT long since a friend said to me, "Growing old is the
saddest thing in the world." Since then I have been
thinking about growing old, trying to decide if I thought her
right. But I cannot agree with her. True, we lose some things
that we prize as time passes and acquire a few that we
would prefer to be without. But we may gain infinitely more
with the years than we lose in wisdom, character, and the
sweetness of life.

As to the ills of old age, it may be that those of the past were
as bad but are dimmed by the distance. Though old age has
gray hair and twinges of rheumatism, remember that child-
hood has freckles, tonsils and the measles.                  Laura Ingalls Wilder

A FTER bathing him, Fermina Daza helped him to dress:
she sprinkled talcum powder between his legs, she
smoothed cocoa butter on his rashes, she helped him put
on his undershorts with as much love as if they had been
a diaper, and continued dressing him, item by item, from
his socks to the knot in his tie with the topaz pin. Their
conjugal dawns grew calm because he had returned to
the childhood his children had taken away from him. And
she, in turn, at last accepted the domestic schedule because
the years were passing for her too; she slept less and less,
and by the time she was seventy she was awake before       Gabriel García
her husband.                                                Márquez

IN a Cree tale a woman married to a pond speaks to her husband by the way she swims in him. There comes a time when there's no rain and the pond dries up. The woman sets off looking for her husband and, after many miles, finds him in a hole. She takes him home little by little in her hands.

Elizabeth Hay

HOW do I love thee? Let me count the ways.
I love thee to the depth and breadth and height
My soul can reach, when feeling out of sight
For the ends of Being and ideal Grace.
I love thee to the level of every day's
Most quiet need, by sun and candlelight.
I love thee freely, as men strive for Right;
I love thee purely, as they turn from Praise;
I love thee with the passion put to use
In my old griefs, and with my childhood's faith.
I love thee with a love I seemed to lose
With my lost saints — I love thee with the breath,
Smiles, tears of all my life! — and, if God choose,
I shall but love thee better after death.

Elizabeth Barrett
Browning
Nineteenth century

GRANT, we beseech thee, O Lord our God, that in whatever dangers we are placed we may call upon thy name, and that when deliverance is given us from on high we may never cease from thy praise; through Jesus Christ our Lord.

Leonine Sacramentary

Pardon the faults in me,
   for the love of years ago:
      Good bye.
I must drift across the sea,
   I must sink into the snow,
      I must die.

You can bask in this sun,
   You can drink wine, and eat:
      Good bye.
I must gird myself and run,
   Tho' with unready feet:
      I must die.

Blank sea to sail upon,
   Cold bed to sleep in:
      Good bye.
While you clasp, I must be gone
   For all your weeping:
      I must die.

A kiss for one friend,
   and a word for two, —
      Good bye: —
A lock that you must send,
   a kindness you must do:
      I must die.

Not a word for you,
   Not a lock or kiss,
      Good bye.
We, one, must part in two;
   Verily death is this:
      I must die.

Christina Rossetti
Nineteenth century

Mishna

RABBI Johanan said: If a man's first wife dies, it is as if the Temple were destroyed in his day. Rabbi Alexandri said: If a man's wife dies, the world becomes dark for him. Rabbi Samuel ben Nahman said: For everything there is a substitute except for the wife of one's youth.

Helen Bevington

I don't feel like a survivor. I feel left behind.

I want to die while you love me,
While yet you hold me fair,
While laughter lies upon my lips
And lights are in my hair.

I want to die while you love me,
I could not bear to see,

The glory of this perfect day,
Grown dim — or cease to be.

I want to die while you love me,
Oh! who could care to live
Till love has nothing more to ask,
and nothing more to give.

I want to die while you love me,
And bear to that still bed
Your kisses, turbulent, unspent,
To warm me when I'm dead.

Georgia Douglas
Johnson

THE cloth-plant grew till it covered the thorn bush;
The bindweed spread over the wilds.
My lovely one is here no more.
With whom? No, I sit alone.

Summer days, winter nights —
Year after year of them must pass
Till I go to him where he dwells.
Winter nights, summer days —
Year after year of them must pass
Till I go to his home.

Chou song
Seventh century BCE

LAUGHTER is thine, the laughter free from scorn,
And thine the smile upon a cheerful face:
Thine, too, the tears, when love for love must mourn,
And death brings silence for a little space.
Thou gavest, and thou dost not take away:
The parting is but here, and for a day.

Fullness of life, in body, mind, and soul;
"Who saves his life shall lose it," thou hast said:
A great adventure with a glorious goal;
Nothing that lives in thee is ever dead:
Brave living here: and then, beyond the grave,
More life and more adventure for the brave.

Godfrey Fox Bradby

SHE prayed to God to give him at least a moment so that
he would not go without knowing how much she had
loved him despite all their doubts, and she felt an irre-
sistible longing to begin life with him over again so that
they could say what they had left unsaid and do everything
right that they had done badly in the past. But she had to
give in to the intransigence of death.

Gabriel García
Márquez

S HE had wanted him to live so much and he was dead.
No hour is ever eternity, but it has its right to weep. Janie
held his head tightly to her breast and wept and thanked
him wordlessly for giving her the chance for loving service.

Zora Neale Hurston

I knew you'd never leave me, something the physician
who would not let me hold your dead hand
failed to understand. He was trying to separate
the living woman from the dead man and did not know
the living and the dead never let go.
Simply because they don't have to.
So when I lift your green T-shirt from the drawer
to feel your body's smells or when you speak
to me in my dreams, never think I am ungrateful.
But even with the sweetness of nothing, flesh longs
for its kind. The next time your spirit walks
the house, if you'd stop, hold still
and let me come to you, hold your hand in mine,
that, my love, would be a miracle.

Laurie Duesing

G IVE us strength in sorrow, want or pain,
Always steadfast to remain.
And when clouds shall fill our skies of blue,
Help our love to see us through.
Oh, God, until we reach Life's ebbing tide,
May we in perfect love and peace abide.
And when Life's sun shall set beyond the hill,
May we go hand in hand, together still.

Fern C. Dunlap

IN every room of my house I can see
at least one photograph of him. In the one
I look at now he sits sidesaddle
on his motorcycle, smiling at me.

He was always in motion. But since he died,
I can't stop moving. I am looking
for his body, backlit by the sun. I walk
out to the yard filled with plants

he gave me. Gladiolas spray peach and magenta
into the air. See what you've done,
I say. Nothing can keep me from it.
Everything you gave me is in bloom.

Laurie Duesing

OF course he wasn't dead. He could never be dead
until she herself had finished feeling and thinking.
The kiss of his memory made pictures of love and light
against the wall. Here was peace.

Zora Neale Hurston

WEEP not, weep not,
she is not dead;
She's resting in the bosom of Jesus.
Heart-broken husband — weep no more;
Grief-stricken son — weep no more;
Left-lonesome daughter — weep no more;
She's only just gone home.

James Weldon Johnson

A marriage should begin with God's blessing, proceed in harmony and virtuous living, and finally lead the whole family to the kingdom of heaven.

John Chrysostom
Fourth century

B EYOND all earthly sorrow,
Beyond earth's selfish claim,
I've found a glad tomorrow
And joyfully exclaim,
"O grave, where is thy victory?
O death, where is thy sting?"

Shaker hymn

T HE crowning of the couple in the Byzantine rite captures this well. These are not the crowns of arrogance, or of make-believe princes and princesses, but the crown of martyrs, suggesting that married couples, too, faithful unto death, witness to Christ and make up what is to be made up in his sufferings. In other words, marriage is a pathway to salvation, a crucible for the transformation of faithful souls, a way to eternal life.

Mark Searle

AFTER this I heard what seem to be the loud voice of a
great multitude in heaven, saying,
"Hallelujah!
Salvation and glory and power to our God."

And from the throne came a voice saying,
"Praise our God,
all you his servants,

and all who fear him,
small and great."

Then I heard what seemed to be the voice of a great multitude, like the sound of many waters and like the sound of
mighty thunderpeals, crying out,

"Hallelujah!
For the Lord our God
the Almighty reigns.
Let us rejoice and exult
and give him the glory,
for the marriage of the Lamb has come,
and his bride has made herself ready;
to her it has been granted to be clothed
with fine linen, bright and pure! —
for the fine linen is the righteous deeds of the saints.

And the angel said to me, "Write this: Blessed are those
who are invited to the marriage supper of the Lamb."    Revelation 19:1; 5 – 9a

'TWAS a long Parting — but the time
For Interview — had Come —
Before the Judgment Seat of God —
The last — and second time

These Fleshless Lovers met —
A Heaven in a Gaze —
A Heaven of Heavens — the Privilege
Of one another's Eyes —

No Lifetime — on Them —
Appareled as the new
Unborn — except They had beheld —
Born infiniter — now —

Was Bridal — e'er like This?
A Paradise — the Host —
And Cherubim — and Seraphim —
The unobtrusive Guest —

Emily Dickinson
Nineteenth century

NOT for tongues of heaven's angels,
Not for wisdom to discern,
Not for faith that masters mountains —
For this better gift we yearn:
May love be ours, Lord; may love be ours.
May love be ours, O Lord.

Soon will fade the word of wisdom,
Faith and hope be one day past:
When we see our Savior clearly,
Love it is alone will last —
May love be ours, Lord; may love be ours.

Timothy Dudley-Smith    May love be ours, O Lord.

# Endnotes

## Man and Woman, Woman and Man

**Bone represents strength:** From *Commentaries on the Ritual Readings* by Robert Crotty and John Barry Ryan. Copyright © 1982 by The Liturgical Press. Reprinted with permission of The Liturgical Press, Collegeville, Minnesota.

**The masculine and:** From *The Sacrament of Love: The Nuptial Mystery in the Light of the Orthodox Tradition* by Paul Evdokimov. Copyright © 1985 by St. Vladimir's Seminary Press, 575 Scarsdale Road, Crestwood NY 10707. Used with permission.

**So when she:** From "Song" by William Blake found in *The Penguin Book of English Christian Verse*. Published by Penguin Books Ltd., 1984.

**The bee is:** From *Songs for the Bride* by William G. Archer, 1985, © Columbia University Press, New York. Reprinted with permission of the publisher.

**Our mind's desire:** From *The Reasons of the Heart: A Journey into Solitude and Back Again into the Human Circle* by John S. Dunne. Copyright © 1978 by John S. Dunne. Used by permission of the Macmillan Publishing Company.

**Every deed and:** From *Markings* by Dag Hammar-skjöld, trans., Leif Sjöberg & W. H. Auden. Translation copyright © 1964 by Alfred A. Knopf, Inc., and Faber & Faber Ltd. Reprinted by permission of Alfred A. Knopf.

**Loneliness clarifies. Here:** From *The Whitsun Weddings* by Phillip Larkin. Copyright © 1964 by Phillip Larkin. Reprinted by permission of Random House, Inc.

**God created co-being:** From *The Sacrament of Love: The Nuptial Mystery in the Light of the Orthodox Tradition* by Paul Evdokimov. Copyright © 1985 by St. Vladimir's Seminary Press, 575 Scarsdale Road, Crestwood NY 10707. Used with permission.

**Rabbi Hanilai said:** From *A Rabbinic Anthology* by C. G. Montefiore and H. Lowe, editors. Copyright © 1974 by Schocken Books, Inc. Reprinted by permission of Schocken Books, published by Pantheon Books, a division of Random House, Inc.

**'Tis midnight, but:** From *The Penguin Book of Religious Verse*. Published by Penguin Books Ltd., 1963.

**When the black-lettered:** From "Wife, Children and Friends" by William Robert Spencer. Found in *Bartlett's Familiar Quotations*. Published by Garden City Publishing, 1944.

**Bless, O Lord:** From *To Join Together: The Rite of Marriage* by Kenneth W. Stevenson. Copyright © 1987 by The Liturgical Press. Reprinted with permission of The Liturgical Press, Collegeville, Minnesota.

**The one who:** From *The Sacrament of Love: The Nuptial Mystery in the Light of the Orthodox Tradition* by Paul Evdokimov. Copyright © 1985 by St. Vladimir's Seminary Press, 575 Scarsdale Road, Crestwood NY 10707. Used with permission.

**Love and commitment:** From *Habits of the Heart: Individualism and Commitment in American Life* by Robert Bellah. Copyright © 1985 by the University of California Press. Used with permission of the Regents of the University of California and the University of California Press.

**The overtones are:** From *Markings* by Dag Hammarskjöld, trans., Leif Sjöberg & W. H. Auden. Translation copyright © 1964 by Alfred A. Knopf, Inc., and Faber & Faber Ltd. Reprinted by permission of Alfred A. Knopf.

**Strange atoms we:** "Lovelight" by Georgia Douglas Johnson. Reprinted from *American Negro Poetry*, published by Hill and Wang, 1963.

**By the clearing:** From *The Book of Songs* translated by Arthur Waley. Published by Grove/Atlantic, Inc., 1960.

**There are three:** Reprinted with the permission of Atheneum Publishers, an imprint of Macmillan Publishing Company from *Miss Manners' Guide to Excruciatingly Correct Behavior* by Judith Martin. Copyright © 1979, 1980, 1981, 1982 by United Features Syndicates, Inc.

**Love is principally:** From *Sex for the Common Man*. Published by Arno Press, 1974.

**Betrothal was so:** From *To Join Together: The Rite of Marriage* by Kenneth W. Stevenson. Copyright © 1987 by The Liturgical Press. Reprinted with permission of The Liturgical Press, Collegeville, Minnesota.

**Over the southern:** From *The Book of Songs* translated by Arthur Waley. Published by Grove/Atlantic, Inc., 1960.

## In Good Times and in Bad

**He drifted off:** From *Their Eyes Were Watching God* by Zora Neale Hurston. Published by J. B. Lippincott, 1937.

**You begin your:** From *Ritual of Marriage*. Published by Bruce Publishing, 1954.

**Let me finish:** From *Markings* by Dag Hammarskjöld, trans., Leif Sjöberg & W. H. Auden. Translation copyright © 1964 by Alfred A. Knopf, Inc., and Faber & Faber Ltd. Reprinted by permission of Alfred A. Knopf.

## One Flesh

**Lo, brethren, we:** From *Documents of the Marriage Liturgy* by Mark Searle and Kenneth W. Stevenson. Copyright © 1992 by The Liturgical Press. Reprinted with permission of The Liturgical Press, Collegeville, Minnesota.

**At the beginning:** From *To Join Together: The Rite of Marriage* by Kenneth W. Stevenson. Copyright © 1987 by The Liturgical Press. Reprinted with permission of The Liturgical Press, Collegeville, Minnesota.

**Husband and wife:** From *Marriage: East and West* by David and Vera Mace. Published by Dolphin Books, 1960.

**The wedding ring:** From *The Wedding Book* by Howard Kirschenbaum and Rockwell Stensrud. Published by The Seabury Press, 1974.

**Moreover, those who:** From *Documents of the Marriage Liturgy* by Mark Searle and Kenneth W. Stevenson. Copyright © 1992 by The Liturgical Press. Reprinted with permission of The Liturgical Press, Collegeville, Minnesota.

**Yard sale—Recently:** From the *San Jose Mercury News*. Reprinted from *The 637 Best Things Anybody Ever Said,* published by Fawcett Columbine, 1982.

**O perfect Love:** From *The Hymnal of the Protestant Episcopal Church in the U.S.A.,* © 1940 The Church Pension Fund.

**Bless them, O:** From *Documents of the Marriage Liturgy* by Mark Searle and Kenneth W. Stevenson. Copyright © 1992 by The Liturgical Press. Reprinted with permission of The Liturgical Press, Collegeville, Minnesota.

**Thus each new:** From *Documents of the Marriage Liturgy* by Mark Searle and Kenneth W. Stevenson. Copyright © 1992 by The Liturgical Press. Reprinted with permission of The Liturgical Press, Collegeville, Minnesota.

**Marriage belongs to:** From *Theology of Christian Marriage.* Published by The Seabury Press, 1980.

**O may Thy:** From *A Shaker Hymnal.* Published by The Overlook Press, 1990.

**Look down from:** From *The Roman Ritual* translated and edited by the Reverend Philip T. Weller. Published by The Bruce Publishing Company, 1950.

**A group of:** From *The New Jewish Wedding* by Anita Diamant. Copyright © 1985 by Anita Diamant. Reprinted by permission of Simon & Schuster, Inc.

**Alleluia and glory:** From *To Join Together: The Rite of Marriage* by Kenneth W. Stevenson. Copyright © 1987 by The Liturgical Press. Reprinted with permission of The Liturgical Press, Collegeville, Minnesota.

**Praised are you:** From *The New Jewish Wedding* by Anita Diamant. Copyright © 1985 by Anita Diamant. Reprinted by permission of Simon & Schuster, Inc.

**O God, through:** From *Documents of the Marriage Liturgy* by Mark Searle and Kenneth W. Stevenson. Copyright © 1992 by The Liturgical Press. Reprinted with permission of The Liturgical Press, Collegeville, Minnesota.

**You are members:** From *The Roman Ritual* translated and edited by the Reverend Philip T. Weller. Published by The Bruce Publishing Company, 1950.

**With the love:** From *Markings* by Dag Hammarskjöld, trans., Leif Sjöberg & W. H. Auden. Translation copyright © 1964 by Alfred A. Knopf, Inc., and Faber & Faber Ltd. Reprinted by permission of Alfred A. Knopf.

**Whatever regard Christian:** From *The Roman Ritual* translated and edited by the Reverend Philip T. Weller. Published by The Bruce Publishing Company, 1950.

**Our mothers Rebekkah:** From *The New Jewish Wedding* by Anita Diamant. Copyright © 1985 by Anita Diamant. Reprinted by permission of Simon & Schuster, Inc.

**May each have:** From *Documents of the Marriage Liturgy* by Mark Searle and Kenneth W. Stevenson. Copyright © 1992 by The Liturgical Press. Reprinted with permission of The Liturgical Press, Collegeville, Minnesota.

**The foundation for:** From *Commentaries on the Ritual Readings* by Robert Crotty and John Barry Ryan. Copyright © 1982 by The Liturgical Press. Reprinted with permission of The Liturgical Press, Collegeville, Minnesota.

**On those who:** From *The Hymnal of the Protestant Episcopal Church in the U.S.A.,* © 1940 The Church Pension Fund.

**O Lord, who:** From *The Order of Solemnization of the Sacrament of Matrimony.* Copyright © 1972 by Metropolitan Mar Athanasius Yeshue Samuel. Used with permission.

**May the blessing:** From *Documents of the Marriage Liturgy* by Mark Searle and Kenneth W. Stevenson. Copyright © 1992 by The Liturgical Press. Reprinted with permission of The Liturgical Press, Collegeville, Minnesota.

**May we stay:** From *The Prayers of African Religion* by John S. Mbiti. Published by Orbis Books, 1975.

**May all evil:** From *Documents of the Marriage Liturgy* by Mark Searle and Kenneth W. Stevenson. Copyright © 1992 by The Liturgical Press. Reprinted with permission of The Liturgical Press, Collegeville, Minnesota.

**The bridegroom is:** From *The Order of Solemnization of the Sacrament of Matrimony.* Copyright © 1972 by Metropolitan Mar Athanasius Yeshue Samuel. Used with permission.

**She was stretched:** From *Their Eyes Were Watching God* by Zora Neale Hurston. Published by J. B. Lippincott, 1937.

**Normal sex life:** From *The Development of Personality* by C. G. Jung. Copyright © 1954 by Bollingen Foundation, Inc. Published by Pantheon Books, Inc.

**The body of:** From the *New York Times,* July 4, 1979. Reprinted from *The Quotable Quotations Book,* published by Thomas R. Crowell, 1980.

**The fire of:** From *Markings* by Dag Hammarskjöld, trans., Leif Sjöberg & W. H. Auden. Translation copyright © 1964 by Alfred A. Knopf, Inc., and Faber & Faber Ltd. Reprinted by permission of Alfred A. Knopf.

**Love is not:** "The Dream," copyright © 1955 by Theodore Roethke. From *The Collected Poems of Theodore Roethke* by Theodore Roethke. Used by permission of Doubleday, a division of Bantam Doubleday Dell Publishing Group, Inc.

**People should love:** From *On Marriage and Family Life* translated by Catherine P. Roth and David Anderson. Copyright © 1986 by St. Vladimir's Seminary Press, 575 Scarsdale Road, Crestwood NY 10707. Used with permission.

**We become the:** From *The Sacrament of Love: The Nuptial Mystery in the Light of the Orthodox Tradition* by Paul Evdokimov. Copyright © 1985 by

St. Vladimir's Seminary Press, 575 Scarsdale Road, Crestwood NY 10707. Used with permission.

**You are a:** "You Are a Part of Me" by Frank Yerby. Reprinted from *American Negro Poetry,* published by Hill and Wang, 1963.

**Love creates a:** From *Habits of the Heart: Individualism and Commitment in American Life* by Robert Bellah. Copyright © 1985 by the University of California Press. Used with permission of the Regents of the University of California and the University of California Press.

**They were like:** From *The Return of the Native* by Thomas Hardy. Published by New American Library, 1973.

**They come to:** From *On Marriage and Family Life* translated by Catherine P. Roth and David Anderson. Copyright © 1986 by St. Vladimir's Seminary Press, 575 Scarsdale Road, Crestwood NY 10707. Used with permission.

**While it is:** Reprinted by permission of the publishers and the Trustees of Amherst College from *The Poems of Emily Dickinson,* Thomas H. Johnson, ed. Cambridge, Mass.: The Belknap Press of Harvard University Press, Copyright © 1951, 1955, 1979, 1983 by the President and Fellows of Harvard College.

**So they loved:** From "The Phoenix and the Turtle" by William Shakespeare found in *The Penguin Book of English Christian Verse.* Published by Penguin Books Ltd., 1984.

**The candle had:** Reprinted by permission of G. P. Putnam's Sons from *The Joy Luck Club* by Amy Tan. Copyright © 1989 by Amy Tan.

**Let us build:** "The Altar" from *Selected Poems* by Ezra Pound. © 1928, 1948 by Faber & Faber Limited. Used with permission.

**Bless them in:** From *Documents of the Marriage Liturgy* by Mark Searle and Kenneth W. Stevenson. Copyright © 1992 by The Liturgical Press. Reprinted with permission of The Liturgical Press, Collegeville, Minnesota.

## Gift of Married Love

**Lady, Lady, I:** Reprinted with the permission of Atheneum Publishers, an imprint of Macmillan Publishing Company from *The New Negro: Voices of the Harlem Renaissance* by Alain Locke, editor. © 1925 by Albert & Charled Boni, Inc.

**Father, creator of:** From *Documents of the Marriage Liturgy* by Mark Searle and Kenneth W. Stevenson. Copyright © 1992 by The Liturgical Press. Reprinted with permission of The Liturgical Press, Collegeville, Minnesota.

**Let all thy:** From "To a Bride" by Frances Quarles. Found in *Bartlett's Familiar Quotations,* published by Garden City Publishing, 1944.

**After all, the:** From *Love and Mr. Lewisham* by H. G. Wells.

**It was frightening:** From *Baptism of Desire* by Louise Erdrich. Published by Harper & Row, Publishers, Inc., 1989.

**O make these:** From *Documents of the Marriage Liturgy* by Mark Searle and Kenneth W. Stevenson. Copyright © 1992 by The Liturgical Press. Reprinted with permission of The Liturgical Press, Collegeville, Minnesota.

**The brandisht Sword:** From *The Penguin Book of English Christian Verse.* Published by Penguin Books Ltd., 1984.

**Marriage is given:** From *To Join Together: The Rite of Marriage* by Kenneth W. Stevenson. Copyright © 1987 by The Liturgical Press. Reprinted with permission of The Liturgical Press, Collegeville, Minnesota.

**Teyve: Do you:** From *Fiddler on the Roof* lyrics by Sheldon Harnick. Published by Sunbeam Music Corporation, 1964.

**Then they were:** From "Angry" found in *Where Is Here?* by Joyce Carol Oates. Published by The Ontario Review, Inc., 1992.

**In expressing love:** From *The Third and Possibly the Best 637 Things Anybody Ever Said.* Published by Fawcett Columbine, 1986.

**Most merciful God:** From *The Hodder Book of Christian Prayers* compiled by Tony Castle. Published by Hodder & Stoughton, 1986.

**Love does not:** From *The Sacrament of Love: The Nuptial Mystery in the Light of the Orthodox Tradition* by Paul Evdokimov. Copyright © 1985 by St. Vladirnir's Seminary Press, 575 Scarsdale Road, Crestwood NY 10707. Used with permission.

**Beloved of Christ:** From *The Roman Ritual* translated and edited by the Reverend Philip T. Weller. Published by The Bruce Publishing Company, 1950.

**Two souls so:** From *The Sacrament of Love: The Nuptial Mystery in the Light of the Orthodox Tradition* by Paul Evdokimov. Copyright © 1985 by St. Vladimir's Seminary Press, 575 Scarsdale Road, Crestwood NY 10707. Used with permission.

**Because you come:** From "Because" lyrics by Edward Teschemacher. Published by Hal Leonard Publishing Corporation, 1983.

**Grant them, Lord:** From *Documents of the Marriage Liturgy* by Mark Searle and Kenneth W. Stevenson. Copyright © 1992 by The Liturgical Press. Reprinted with permission of The Liturgical Press, Collegeville, Minnesota.

**May the halo:** From *A Shaker Hymnal.* Published by The Overlook Press, 1990.

**Therefore the sacred:** From the *Encyclical Letter On Christian Marriage.* Published by the National Catholic Welfare Conference, 1930.

**So — in the:** From *Markings* by Dag Hammarskjöld, trans., Leif Sjöberg & W. H. Auden. Translation copyright © 1964 by Alfred A. Knopf, Inc., and Faber & Faber Ltd. Reprinted by permission of Alfred A. Knopf.

**Many times a:** "Abraham Tells Ann He Loves Her" from The *Unexamined Wife* by Sherril Jaffe. Copyright © 1983 by Sherril Jaffe.

**When Christians marry:** From *Commentaries on the Ritual Readings* by Robert Crotty and John Barry Ryan. Copyright © 1982 by The Liturgical Press. Reprinted with permission of The Liturgical Press, Collegeville, Minnesota.

## Life in Common

**If, as Paul:** From *Commentaries on the Ritual Readings* by Robert Crotty and John Barry Ryan. Copyright © 1982 by The Liturgical Press. Reprinted with permission of The Liturgical Press, Collegeville, Minnesota.

**Rabbi Jacob said:** From *A Rabbinic Anthology* by C. G. Montefiore and H. Lowe, editors. Copyright © 1974 by Schocken Books, Inc. Reprinted by permission of Schocken Books, published by Pantheon Books, a division of Random House, Inc.

**These are the:** "Two Sides of Calvin," from *Times Three* by Phyllis McGinley. Copyright 1932–1960 by Phyllis McGinley; Copyright 1938–1942, 1944, 1945, 1958, 1959 by The Curtis Publishing Co. Used by permission of Viking Penguin, a division of Penguin Books USA, Inc.

**You can give:** From *Blue Calhoun* by Reynolds Price. Published by Atheneum Books, 1992.

**Love is like:** "Love and Friendship" by Emily Bronte. Reprinted from *Literature: An Introduction to Fiction, Poetry and Drama,* published by Little Brown.

**Holy God, you:** From *Documents of the Marriage Liturgy* by Mark Searle and Kenneth W. Stevenson. Copyright © 1992 by The Liturgical Press. Reprinted with permission of The Liturgical Press, Collegeville, Minnesota.

**It is what:** From *The Reasons of the Heart: A Journey into Solitude and Back Again into the Human Circle* by John S. Dunne. Copyright © 1978 by John S. Dunne. Used by permission of the Macmillan Publishing Company.

**Grant, O heavenly:** From *The Hodder Book of Christian Prayers* compiled by Tony Castle. Published by Hodder & Stoughton, 1986.

## Forgiveness

**Lord, cleanse the:** "Forgive Our Sins" words by Rosamund Herklots. Copyright Oxford University Press.

**Forgiveness does not:** From *Strength to Love* © 1981 by Fortress Press. Used with permission.

**Forgiveness is the:** From *Markings* by Dag Hammarskjöld, trans., Leif Sjöberg & W. H. Auden. Translation copyright © 1964 by Alfred A. Knopf, Inc., and Faber & Faber Ltd. Reprinted by permission of Alfred A. Knopf.

**Nevertheless, since it:** From the *Encyclical Letter On Christian Marriage.* Published by the National Catholic Welfare Conference, 1930.

**Watch yourself, be:** From *Good Wives* by Louisa M. Alcott. Published by J. M. Dent & Sons Ltd., 1979.

**Such a silly:** From *Songs for the Bride* by William G. Archer, 1985. Copyright © Columbia University Press, New York. Reprinted with permission of the publisher.

**Zip, zip the:** From *The Book of Songs* translated by Arthur Waley. Published by Grove/Atlantic Inc., 1960.

**I had vowed:** From *Ordinary Time: Cycles in Marriage, Faith, and Renewal,* © 1993 by Nancy Mairs. Used with permission.

**Even in the:** From *Markings* by Dag Hammarskjöld, trans., Leif Sjöberg & W. H. Auden. Translation copyright © 1964 by Alfred A. Knopf, Inc., and Faber & Faber Ltd. Reprinted by permission of Alfred A. Knopf.

**We are with:** "No Smiles" by Frank Lamont Phillips. Reprinted from *American Negro Poetry,* published by Hill and Wang, 1963.

**Now they were:** From *The Last Tycoon* by F. Scott Fitzgerald. Published by The Bodley Head, 1958.

**Talking in bed:** From *The Whitsun Weddings* by Phillip Larkin. Copyright © 1964 by Phillip Larkin. Reprinted by permission of Random House, Inc.

**Our hearts are:** From *The Hodder Book of Christian Prayers* compiled by Tony Castle. Published by Hodder & Stoughton, 1986.

**When Jane had:** From *Love and Work* by Reynolds Price. Published by Atheneum Books, 1975.

**Like the bee:** From *Markings* by Dag Hammarskjöld, trans., Leif Sjöberg & W. H. Auden. Translation copyright © 1964 by Alfred A. Knopf, Inc., and Faber & Faber Ltd. Reprinted by permission of Alfred A. Knopf.

**The hut is:** From *The Forest People* by Colin M. Turnbull. Published by Simon & Schuster, 1961.

**You say you:** From *The Heart of the Matter* by Graham Greene. Published by Penguin Books Ltd., 1971.

**My dear Eustacia:** From *The Return of the Native* by Thomas Hardy. Permission by New American Library, 1973.

**There is no:** From *Insights: A Talmudic Treasury* by Saul Weiss. Published by Feldheim Publishers, 1990.

**He could not:** From *Anna Karenina* by Leo Tolstoy. Published by W. W. Norton & Company, Inc., 1970.

**When crossed in:** From *Sex for the Common Man.* Published by Arno Press, 1974.

**He knew she'd:** From *Love and Work* by Reynolds Price. Published by Atheneum Books, 1975.

**When my husband:** From *Marriage: East and West* by David and Vera Mace. Published by Dolphin Books, 1960.

**Still, it is:** "Flags" from "Blacks," published by Third World Press, Chicago; by Gwendolyn Brooks, © 1991. Used with permission.

**A good argument:** From *When You Look Like Your Passport Photo, It's Time to Go Home* by Erma Bombeck. Published by HarperCollins, 1991.

## A Sign of Christ's Love

**The house of:** From *The Order of Solemnization of the Sacrament of Matrimony.* Copyright © 1972 by Metropolitan Mar Athanasius Yeshue Samuel. Used with permission.

**We bless you:** From *Documents of the Marriage Liturgy* by Mark Searle and Kenneth W. Stevenson. Copyright © 1992 by The Liturgical Press. Reprinted with permission of The Liturgical Press, Collegeville, Minnesota.

**We also pledge:** From *The New Jewish Wedding* by Anita Diamant. Copyright © 1985 by Anita Diamant. Reprinted by permission of Simon & Schuster, Inc.

**The earthly love:** From *The Roman Ritual* translated and edited by the Reverend Philip T. Weller. Published by The Bruce Publishing Company, 1950.

**In its full:** From *The Sacrament of Love: The Nuptial Mystery in the Light of the Orthodox Tradition* by Paul Evdokimov. Copyright © 1985 by St. Vladimir's Seminary Press, 575 Scarsdale Road, Crestwood NY 10707. Used with permission.

**Marriage, like monasticism:** From *On Marriage and Family Life* translated by Catherine P. Roth and David Anderson. Copyright © 1986 by St. Vladimir's Seminary Press, 575 Scarsdale Road, Crestwood NY 10707. Used with permission.

**Marriage is a:** From *The Roman Ritual* translated and edited by the Reverend Philip T. Weller. Published by The Bruce Publishing Company, 1950.

**Our Lord Jesus:** From *The Order of Solemnization of the Sacrament of Matrimony.* Copyright © 1972 by Metropolitan Mar Athanasius Yeshue Samuel. Used with permission.

**Unique to the:** From *Documents of the Marriage Liturgy* by Mark Searle and Kenneth W. Stevenson. Copyright © 1992 by The Liturgical Press. Reprinted with permission of The Liturgical Press, Collegeville, Minnesota.

**It is you:** From *The Sacrament of Love: The Nuptial Mystery in the Light of the Orthodox Tradition* by Paul Evdokimov. Copyright © 1985 by St. Vladimir's Seminary Press, 575 Scarsdale Road, Crestwood NY 10707. Used with permission.

**The settling of:** From *The Sacrament of Love: The Nuptial Mystery in the Light of the Orthodox Tradition* by Paul Evdokimov. Copyright © 1985 by St. Vladimir's Seminary Press, 575 Scarsdale Road, Crestwood NY 10707. Used with permission.

**After the clouds:** From "Reconnaissance" by Arna Bontemps. Copyright © 1963 by Arna Bontemps. Used by permission of Harold Ober Associates, Incorporated.

**To believe a:** From *A La Recharche du Temps Perdu* by Marcel Proust. Published by Bibliotheque de la Pleiade, 1940.

**For this is:** From *A Grief Observed.* Reprinted by permission of Faber & Faber Limited. (published in the United States by Seabury Press).

**In the catacombs:** From *The Sacrament of Love: The Nuptial Mystery in the Light of the Orthodox Tradition* by Paul Evdokimov. Copyright © 1985 by St. Vladimir's Seminary Press, 575 Scarsdale Road, Crestwood NY 10707. Used with permission.

**There were pure:** From *Love and Work* by Reynolds Price. Published by Atheneum Books, 1975.

**Lord, behold our:** From *The Hodder Book of Christian Prayers* compiled by Tony Castle. Published by Hodder & Stoughton, 1986.

## The Gift and Heritage of Children

**Bless them who:** From *Documents of the Marriage Liturgy* by Mark Searle and Kenneth W. Stevenson. Copyright © 1992 by The Liturgical Press. Reprinted with permission of The Liturgical Press, Collegeville, Minnesota.

**The child born:** From *The Sacrament of Love: The Nuptial Mystery in the Light of the Orthodox Tradition* by Paul Evdokimov. Copyright © 1985 by St. Vladimir's Seminary Press, 575 Scarsdale Road, Crestwood NY 10707. Used with permission.

**These are the:** From *On Marriage and Family Life* translated by Catherine P. Roth and David Anderson. Copyright © 1986 by St. Vladimir's Seminary Press, 575 Scarsdale Road, Crestwood NY 10707. Used with permission.

**Marriage: that I:** From *Thus Spake Zarathustra* translated by R. J. Hollingdale. Published by Penguin Books, Ltd., 1969.

**The crowning also:** From *Parents and Priests as Servants of Redemption* by Athenagoras Kokkinakis. Published by Morehouse-Goreham Co., 1958.

**Christ was invited:** From *The Roman Ritual* translated and edited by the Reverend Philip T. Weller. Published by The Bruce Publishing Company, 1950.

**Up the stairs:** From *The Souls of Black Folk* by W. E. B. DuBois. Found in *Three Negro Classics,* published by Avon Books, 1965.

**Let the sweetness:** From *Documents of the Marriage Liturgy* by Mark Searle and Kenneth W. Stevenson. Copyright © 1992 by The Liturgical Press. Reprinted with permission of The Liturgical Press, Collegeville, Minnesota.

**Because of their:** From *Little House in the Ozarks* by Laura Ingalls Wilder. Copyright © 1991 by Stephen W. Hines. Used with permission of Thomas Nelson, Inc.

**Through their devout:** From the *Encyclical Letter On Christian Marriage.* Published by the National Catholic Welfare Conference, 1930.

**The Israelites say:** From *A Rabbinic Anthology* by C. G. Montefiore and H. Lowe, editors. Copyright © 1974 by Schocken Books, Inc. Reprinted by permission of Schocken Books, published by Pantheon Books, a division of Random House, Inc.

**Across the years:** From *Little House in the Ozarks* by Laura Ingalls Wilder. Copyright © 1991 by Stephen W. Hines. Used with permission of Thomas Nelson, Inc.

**You have joined:** From *Documents of the Marriage Liturgy* by Mark Searle and Kenneth W. Stevenson. Copyright © 1992 by The Liturgical Press. Reprinted with permission of The Liturgical Press, Collegeville, Minnesota.

**May your life:** From *Documents of the Marriage Liturgy* by Mark Searle and Kenneth W. Stevenson. Copyright © 1992 by The Liturgical Press. Reprinted with permission of The Liturgical Press, Collegeville, Minnesota.

**Let us join:** From *Marriage: East and West* by David and Vera Mace. Published by Dolphin Books, 1960.

**May they be:** From *The Prayers of African Religion* by John S. Mbiti. Published by Orbis Books, 1975.

**After Sam was:** From *Heartburn* by Nora Ephron. Published by Alfred A. Knopf, Inc., 1983.

**A man can't:** From *The Third and Possibly the Best 637 Things Anybody Ever Said.* Published by Fawcett Columbine, 1986.

**Your own offspring:** From *Insights: A Talmudic Treasury* by Saul Weiss. Published by Feldheim Publishers, 1990.

**So sturdy and:** From *The Souls of Black Folk* by W. E. B. DuBois. Found in *Three Negro Classics,* published by Avon Books, 1965.

**I loved all:** From *Brothers and Keepers* by John Edgar Wideman. Published by Penguin Books Ltd., 1984.

## Love and Concern for Others

**Marriage is also:** From *To Join Together: The Rite of Marriage* by Kenneth W. Stevenson. Copyright © 1987 by The Liturgical Press. Reprinted with permission of The Liturgical Press, Collegeville, Minnesota.

**A couple that:** From *Commentaries on the Ritual Readings* by Robert Crotty and John Barry Ryan. Copyright © 1982 by The Liturgical Press. Reprinted with permission of The Liturgical Press, Collegeville, Minnesota.

**True love is:** From *The Sacrament of Love: The Nuptial Mystery in the Light of the Orthodox Tradition* by Paul Evdokimov. Copyright © 1985 by St. Vladimir's Seminary Press, 575 Scarsdale Road, Crestwood NY 10707. Used with permission.

**The renewal of:** From *Documents of the Marriage Liturgy* by Mark Searle and Kenneth W. Stevenson. Copyright © 1992 by The Liturgical Press. Reprinted with permission of The Liturgical Press, Collegeville, Minnesota.

**Nothing if not:** "So?" by James P. Vaughn. Reprinted from *American Negro Poetry,* published by Hill and Wang, 1963.

**The groom and:** From *The New Jewish Wedding* by Anita Diamant. Copyright © 1985 by Anita Diamant. Reprinted by permission of Simon & Schuster, Inc.

**Go work in:** From *A Shaker Hymnal.* Published by The Overlook Press, 1990.

**Dear Lord! kind:** From *The Hodder Book of Christian Prayers* compiled by Tony Castle. Published by Hodder & Stoughton, 1986.

**Of all the:** "Wife" by Norman Fischer. Copyright © 1992 by Norman Fischer.

**May the peace:** From *The Rites of the Catholic Church.* Copyright © 1976, 1983 by The Liturgical Press. Reprinted by Permission of The Liturgical Press, Collegeville, Minnesota.

**Give us, Lord:** From *The Hodder Book of Christian Prayers* compiled by Tony Castle. Published by Hodder & Stoughton, 1986.

**If you are:** From *On Marriage and Family Life* translated by Catherine P. Roth and David Anderson. Copyright © 1986 by St. Vladimir's Seminary Press, 575 Scarsdale Road, Crestwood NY 10707. Used with permission.

**Fill my house:** From "Fill my house" by Peter Kearney. Copyright © 1966, J. Albert & Son Pty. Used with permission.

**O living bread:** From *The Hodder Book of Christian Prayers* compiled by Tony Castle. Published by Hodder & Stoughton, 1986.

**The love of:** From *On Marriage and Family Life* translated by Catherine P. Roth and David Anderson. Copyright © 1986 by St. Vladimir's Seminary Press, 575 Scarsdale Road, Crestwood NY 10707. Used with permission.

**Lord, in their:** "Rogation" found in *The Hymnal of the Protestant Episcopal Church.* Copyright Oxford University Press.

**Fill their houses:** From *Documents of the Marriage Liturgy* by Mark Searle and Kenneth W. Stevenson. Copyright © 1992 by The Liturgical Press. Reprinted with permission of The Liturgical Press, Collegeville, Minnesota.

**Gratitude and readiness:** From *Markings* by Dag Hammarskjöld, trans., Leif Sjöberg & W. H. Auden. Translation copyright © 1964 by Alfred A. Knopf, Inc., and Faber & Faber Ltd. Reprinted by permission of Alfred A. Knopf.

**If God loves:** From "Pray Without Ceasing" by Wendall Berry. From *Fidelity* by Wendall Berry. Published by Pantheon Books, 1992.

## Aging and Death

**Grow old along:** From "Rabbi Ben Ezra" by Robert Browning found in *The Penguin Book of Religious Verse.* Published by Penguin Books Ltd., 1963.

**Grant them to:** From *To Join Together: The Rite of Marriage* by Kenneth W. Stevenson. Copyright © 1987 by The Liturgical Press. Reprinted with permission of The Liturgical Press, Collegeville, Minnesota.

**For every generation:** From *The New Jewish Wedding* by Anita Diamant. Copyright © 1985 by Anita Diamant. Reprinted by permission of Simon & Schuster, Inc.

**Look down, O:** From *Documents of the Marriage Liturgy* by Mark Searle and Kenneth W. Stevenson. Copyright © 1992 by The Liturgical Press. Reprinted with permission of The Liturgical Press, Collegeville, Minnesota.

**On the day:** From *The Roman Ritual* translated and edited by the Reverend Philip T. Weller. Copyright © 1950 by The Bruce Publishing Company.

**Today is the:** By Berta Mae Hall Woods. Used by permission of her children.

**When you came:** "A Decade," from *The Complete Poetical Works of Amy Lowell.* Copyright © 1955 by Houghton Mifflin Company, © renewed 1983 by Houghton Mifflin Company, Brinton P. Roberts, and G. D'Andelot Belin, Esquire. Reprinted by permission of Houghton Mifflin Company. All rights reserved.

**If ever two:** From *The New Oxford Book of Christian Verse* edited by Donald Davie. Published by Oxford University Press, 1981.

**Think we have:** From *All for Love in John Dryden: selected works.* Published by Holt, Rinehart and Winston, 1971.

**But in the:** "The Old-Marrieds" from "Blacks," published by Third World Press, Chicago; by Gwendolyn Brooks, © 1991. Used with permission.

**I have seen:** From "The Sweetest Sight that I Have Seen" by Oscar Hammerstein. Copyright © 1944, 1945 by Williamson Music. Used with permission.

**Wish for nothing:** From *Collected Poems* by W. H. Auden. Copyright © 1940 and renewed 1968 by W. H. Auden. Reprinted by permission of Random House, Inc.

**Here from the:** "The Tally Stick" by Jarold Ramsey. Copyright © 1994 by Jarold Ramsey. Used with permission.

**I am glad:** From *Airs from the Woodwinds* by Bessie Calhoun Bird. Reprinted from *Black Sister,* published by Indiana University Press, 1981.

**He was aware:** From *Love in the Time of Cholera* by Gabriel García Márquez, trans., Edith Grossman. Copyright © 1988 by Alfred A. Knopf, Inc. Reprinted by permission of the publisher.

**Now, children, years:** From "Love's Anniversaries (for Joyce)" by Maurice Lindsay. From *Collected Poems* copyright © 1979 by Maurice Lindsay.

**The moon throws:** From *Facing Nature* by John Updike. Copyright © 1985 by John Updike. Reprinted by permission of Alfred A. Knopf Inc.

**Like us, the:** "Pumpkin Lust" by Hunt Hawkins. Reprinted from *The Domestic Life* by Hunt Hawkins, by permission of the University of Pittsburgh Press. Copyright © 1994 by Hunt Hawkins.

**Not long since:** From *Little House in the Ozarks* by Laura Ingalls Wilder. Copyright © 1991 by Stephen W. Hines. Used with permission of Thomas Nelson, Inc.

**After bathing him:** From *Love in the Time of Cholera* by Gabriel García Márquez, trans., Edith Grossman. Copyright © 1988 by Alfred A. Knopf Inc. Reprinted by permission of the publisher.